# 200 GLUTEN-FREE RECIPES

HAMLYN **ALL COLOUR COOKBOOK**

# 200
## GLUTEN-FREE
## RECIPES

An Hachette UK Company
www.hachette.co.uk

First published in Great Britain in 2011 by Hamlyn
a division of Octopus Publishing Group Ltd,
Carmelite House, 50 Victoria Embankment,
London EC4Y 0DZ
www.octopusbooks.co.uk

This edition published in 2016

ISBN 978-0-600-63342-6

A CIP catalogue record for this book is available
from the British Library

Printed and bound in China

10 9 8 7 6 5 4 3 2 1

Standard level spoon measurement are used in all recipes.
1 tablespoon = one 15 ml spoon
1 teaspoon = one 5 ml spoon

Both imperial and metric measures have been given in all
recipes. Use one set of measurements only and not a mixture
of both.

Eggs should be medium unless otherwise stated. The
Department of Health advises that eggs should not be
consumed raw. This book contains dishes made with raw or
lightly cooked eggs. It is prudent for more vulnerable people
such as pregnant and nursing mothers, invalids, the elderly,
babies and young children to avoid uncooked or lightly cooked
dishes made with eggs. Once prepared these dishes should be
kept refrigerated and used promptly.

Ovens should be preheated to the specific temperature – if
using a fan-assisted oven, follow the manufacturer's instructions
for adjusting the time and the temperature.

This book includes dishes made with nuts and nut derivatives.
It is advisable for customers with known allergic reactions to nuts
and nut derivatives and those who may be potentially vulnerable
to these allergies, such as pregnant and nursing mothers,
invalids, the elderly, babies and children, to avoid dishes made
with nuts and nut oils. It is also prudent to check the labels
of pre-prepared ingredients for the possible inclusion of nut
derivatives.

# contents

# introduction

# introduction

This book aims to show you that cooking for someone with coeliac disease need not be difficult or daunting. With careful label checking, combined with the recipes contained here, you will be able to prepare and enjoy a huge range of dishes and goodies – from soups and starters to mains, desserts and cakes and bakes. Gluten-free alternatives exist for recipes you might yearn for, like bread and biscuits. The meals, snacks and treats can all be used as part of a meal plan, and you will find something for all the day's meals whether it's breakfast, lunch, dinner or dessert. With practice, gluten-free cooking will become easier as you get to grips with your repertoire of recipes.

## what is gluten?

Gluten is a type of protein found in a number of grains including wheat, barley and rye. It can also be found in oats if they are processed in the same place as wheat, barley and rye products and have become cross-contaminated. As well as this method of cross-contamination, a few people with coeliac disease are also sensitive to pure, uncontaminated oats. Although these do not contain gluten, they contain a protein that is closely related, therefore many people with coeliac disease choose to eliminate oats from their diet, too.

Gluten gives elasticity to dough, helping it to rise and to keep its shape, and can give the final product a chewy texture. As grains containing gluten are often the main ingredient in many popular food items, such as breads, cakes, many processed foods and cereal goods, finding gluten-free alternatives can be challenging. If you experience an oversensitivity to gluten, which often results in unpleasant symptoms, eliminating these products from your diet is a crucial part of food shopping, preparation and cooking.

## what is coeliac disease?

Coeliac disease is the condition most often associated with an oversensitivity to gluten that causes inflammation in the lining of the small intestine (part of the gut). Coeliac disease is not a food allergy or a food intolerance; it is an autoimmune disease whereby the body makes antibodies against the gluten protein. Antibodies that are usually responsible for attacking bacteria and viruses see the gluten and attack it, in turn causing the inflammation of the lining of the small intestine.

## causes, symptoms and long-term problems

The lining of the small intestine is covered with millions of finger-like projections called villi. When antibodies attack the gluten they cause inflammation, which in turn flattens the villi, meaning that nutrients from food cannot be so readily absorbed. This can result in deficiencies including anaemia.

Other symptoms range from mild to severe and can include diarrhoea, bloating, abdominal pain, excess wind and tiredness, or weakness. Often the symptoms of coeliac disease are confused with irritable bowel syndrome (IBS) or a wheat intolerance, as they manifest themselves similarly. Symptoms can also vary from person to person: in infants coeliac disease presents as a failure to thrive; in children it can cause a lack of appetite, altered bowel habits and anaemia; and within the adult population symptoms include anaemia, diarrhoea, chronic tiredness and lethargy, weight loss and other abdominal abnormalities. Other body systems can also be affected through headaches, hair loss, tooth enamel erosion and joint pain. Long-term

problems caused by untreated or undiagnosed coeliac disease can result in the following:-

- Infertility in women, including recurrent miscarriage
- Poor growth of babies during pregnancy
- Osteoporosis – thinning of bones
- An increased risk of bowel cancer, intestinal lymphoma and cancer of the oesophagus.

A gluten-free diet reduces complications as well as other associated conditions such as mouth ulcers and dermatitis herpetiformis. Sticking to a gluten-free diet will see the risk of any cancers associated with coeliac disease reduced and brought in line with statistics for the normal population.

## who suffers from coeliac disease?

Almost 1 in 100 people in the UK are affected by coeliac disease, but it is thought that at least 60 per cent remain undiagnosed. Anyone, at any age, can develop coeliac disease and it is most commonly diagnosed in people aged between 40 and 50. About 1 in 4 cases are first diagnosed in people aged over 60. Coeliac disease can be hereditary – if you have a close family member who has coeliac disease, then you have a 1 in 10 chance of having or developing coeliac disease. If you have another autoimmune disease – for example, some thyroid diseases, rheumatoid arthritis and type 1 diabetes – then you are also more predisposed to having or developing coeliac disease.

## diagnosis and treatment

If you suspect that you have coeliac disease, don't remove gluten from your diet immediately. First of all, consult your doctor, who will carry out a simple blood test to detect if the antibody against gluten is present. If this blood test is positive, you may be referred for a biopsy of the lining of the small intestine to see if the tell-tale signs of coeliac disease are present. Cutting out gluten before you are tested for coeliac disease may give a negative result.

If you test positive then the next step is to completely cut out gluten from your diet for life. Symptoms will usually disappear within a couple of weeks and the small intestine will begin to repair itself. Symptoms will return, however, even if only a tiny amount of gluten is consumed. Your doctor should refer you to a dietitian who can give you advice on how to deal with coeliac disease and what you should and shouldn't eat. Coeliac UK (www. coeliac.org.uk) is another important port of call – it provides not only advice but also a Food and Drink Directory that lists all gluten-free foods. Manufacturers occasionally change ingredients or suppliers and therefore a product that was previously gluten-free may change to contain gluten. Coeliac UK updates its lists monthly so that you are able to keep up to date with any changes.

In the UK, gluten-free food is available on prescription for people with coeliac disease. These foods are generally staples in the diet, such as bread and pasta, rather than biscuits and cake items. Remember that left untreated, coeliac disease can cause anaemia and osteoporosis, so don't just ignore it.

## following a gluten-free diet

Bearing in mind that gluten is present in all wheat, barley and rye products, and very often in oats through cross-contamination, careful thought needs to be given to shopping for, preparing and cooking a gluten-free diet.

Most manufacturers label products that are gluten-free and may use the Crossed Grain symbol, or their version of this symbol. Even if the packaging doesn't show you the information in this way, looking at the list of ingredients will identify if any products containing gluten are used.

Some foods that contain gluten are obvious – breads, cakes, pastries, biscuits and pasta, for instance. Others, such as processed foods including some soups, crisps and sausages, may also contain gluten, so a good study of food labels is essential. But don't panic! Take a look round at all the wonderful foods that are naturally gluten-free (see right) and you will see that these can be used to make delicious meals. A quick read through the recipes in this book will also reveal that gluten-free cooking can still be exciting, simple, easy and delicious.

### foods that are naturally gluten-free

- Fruits and vegetables, including potatoes
- Unprocessed meat, poultry and fish (including shellfish)
- Unprocessed cheeses, butter, milk and plain milk products including cream
- Eggs
- Tofu
- Cooking oils
- Sugar, bicarbonate of soda, cream of tartar and yeast

- Plain nuts, seeds and pulses
- Rice and its products, such as rice noodles and rice flour (shown on page 11)
- Gluten-free grains and their products, such as buckwheat noodles, polenta and cornflour*
- Natural yogurt
- Vinegars
- Fats
- Coffee and tea
- Herbs and spices

*NB: Some naturally gluten-free grains are milled with wheat, barley and rye, and therefore may be cross-contaminated.

## foods that contain gluten
- Wheat, barley and rye and their products, such as pasta, wheat noodles, bulgar wheat and couscous
- Breads, cakes, biscuits, breakfast cereals and snacks/confectionery containing wheat, barley and rye flour
- Baking powder
- Foods covered in batter, breadcrumbs or dusted with flour
- All beers, stouts, lagers and ales
- Barley water/squash and malted milk drinks
- Some mustard products may contain wheat as a thickener
- Chinese soy sauce, which is traditionally made from fermented wheat
- Stuffing mixes
- Some ready-made seasonings, sauces, soups, gravy granules and stock cubes
- Some sausages contain wheat husk

## gluten-free shop-bought alternatives
As well as the basic foodstuffs that are gluten-free, you can also buy pre-prepared food items that use gluten-free ingredients as a substitute for those containing gluten. Looking round on the supermarket shelves you will see an ever-increasing range of gluten-free products, such as breads, biscuits and pasta, and many of these products have come a long way from the bland, poor-quality gluten-free foods of years gone by.

Gluten-free products are not always quite the same as traditional goods, however, as it is gluten that gives bread its elasticity and cakes their spring. If you try one product and don't like it, don't despair — try another brand or get baking yourself! You will be surprised when you sample some of the carefully selected recipes in this book that use gluten-free ingredients can replicate fairly closely many of the foods that contain gluten.

# store-cupboard essentials

As mentioned before, there are many naturally gluten-free products such as unprocessed meat and fish, dairy foods, fresh fruit and vegetables, rice and pulses. However, you will need to prepare other common foods that are not normally gluten-free – such as white sauce, gravy, cakes, breads and pasta and noodle dishes – using gluten-free ingredients. If you look out for and stock up on some of the following items you will be able to make all the recipes in this book whenever you wish.

### flours

As well as certain flour mixes, there are other gluten-free flours that can be used for baking and cooking, such as rice, chickpea, potato, soya, corn, buckwheat and millet. If these are not available in your local supermarket, they can usually be found in health-food stores or can be ordered online. You don't need to buy them all, however – for general all-purpose use, I find rice flour a great all-rounder and cornflour is good for sauces and thickening in stews, although it is worth experimenting with other flours as well. This book uses rice flour and cornflour primarily.

### xanthan gum

A powder that greatly aids gluten-free baking, xanthan gum, to some extent, replaces the elastic qualities that gluten-free flours lack. Adding a little to gluten-free flours makes bread less crumbly and gluten-free pastry easier to roll and handle. It's available in

specialist health-food stores and in some supermarkets. I have only used xanthan gum in these recipes where it is really needed, opting to use a variety or mix of other flours to get the best results. It is often used in bread recipes, scones, as well as cakes and biscuits.

### gluten-free baking powder

Standard baking powder contains gluten. Gluten-free baking powder is now widely available in the baking sections of supermarkets. Bicarbonate of soda and cream of tartar are naturally gluten-free, so if you prefer to make your own gluten-free baking powder, simply mix 2 parts bicarbonate of soda with 1 part cream of tartar and use this spoon for spoon.

### pasta and noodles

Gluten-free pastas are becoming more common, and are marketed as such. Rice noodles are gluten-free, as are the varieties of soba noodles that are made entirely from buckwheat.

### grains

Quinoa is a brilliant addition to the diet, providing an excellent source of protein as well as being gluten-free. It is a great substitute for couscous or bulgar wheat in salads and side dishes. Polenta is good for baking and for use as an alternative coating to breadcrumbs. As a form of carbohydrate, it can also be used in place of pasta with meals.

### pulses

Lentils and beans can be used in stews and casseroles, but are also great in salads or as side dishes.

### cheese and dairy

Unprocessed cheeses are gluten-free and brilliant to have on hand in the refrigerator; don't overindulge, though, as they are high in fat! Milk and plain, unflavoured yogurts are gluten-free, and it is worth looking at the labels of other dairy products to find gluten-free options.

As with all types of cooking, gluten-free cooking can be a case of trial and error, as gluten-free products have different baking qualities and properties. Don't give up if you find that you don't instantly get good results – you will achieve acceptable results eventually. As well as satisfying a gluten-free diet, the rest of the family will also be more than happy with the recipes in this book.

## cross-contamination

So you have cut out gluten, found your way round the gluten-free products available and have the gluten-free foods list to hand (see page 11–12) … all should be plain sailing from here. You and others around you must be aware, however, that cross-contamination is easy: by spreading butter that has been contaminated with 'normal' breadcrumbs on your gluten-free toast; by using the same toaster for gluten-free and 'normal' bread; or by stirring a gluten-free dish with a spoon that has been stirring gravy made with wheat flour. Even small amounts of gluten can cause the symptoms of coeliac disease to return. Make the following simple but important tips a part of your routine in order to prevent cross-contamination:

### in the home

- Store gluten-free flours separately
- Use separate spoons and knives to prepare gluten-free food
- Keep a 'gluten-free' sieve, rolling pin, pastry brush and chopping board
- Wash everything well and clean surfaces before cooking and eating

### eating out

Check the menu of restaurants where you plan to eat and make sure that staff are aware of your condition prior to your visit. Hidden gluten can be in sauces, coatings (for example, breadcrumbs), gravy and stock cubes. Many chefs are happy to cook you something off the menu with your advice.

## making mistakes

When you have eaten gluten by mistake, you usually start to have some symptoms a few hours after eating and the effects can last from a few hours to several days depending on your sensitivity to what you have eaten. You may want to treat the symptoms or prefer to wait until they naturally get better. If you are experiencing diarrhoea or are vomiting, it is important to keep yourself well hydrated by drinking lots of water. Some people also find that taking medication to treat constipation, diarrhoea or headaches can ease symptoms, so speak to your pharmacist or GP. The most important thing is to get back onto your gluten-free diet as soon as possible to try to prevent further symptoms. If your symptoms are very severe or do not improve, you should discuss this with your GP.

# breakfasts

# homemade muesli

Preparation time **5 minutes**
Cooking time **20 minutes**,
   plus cooling
Serves **4**

100 g (3½ oz) **shredded
   dried coconut**
250 g (8 oz) **buckwheat
   flakes**
250 g (8 oz) **millet flakes**
100 g (3½ oz) **flaked
   almonds**
100 g (3½ oz) **blanched
   hazelnuts**
100 g (3½ oz) **sunflower
   seeds**
100 g (3½ oz) **dried mango**,
   sliced
100 g (3½ oz) **sultanas**

**Spread** the coconut out in a thin layer on a baking sheet. Toast in a preheated oven, 150°C (300°F), Gas Mark 2, for about 20 minutes, stirring every 5 minutes to make sure it browns evenly. Toast the flaked almonds, hazelnuts and sunflower seeds in the same way, but be careful not to allow the seeds to burn. Leave to cool, then roughly chop the hazelnuts.

**Mix** together all the ingredients in a large bowl until well combined. Store in an airtight container for up to 1–2 weeks.

**For Bircher muesli**, mix together the millet flakes, dried mango and sultanas with 1 cored and grated red apple in a large bowl. Pour over 300 ml (½ pint) apple juice, cover and chill overnight. Stir in 200 g (7 oz) toasted and roughly chopped mixed nuts, 125 ml (4 fl oz) natural yogurt and a good drizzle of runny honey before serving.

# granola with berry compote

Preparation time **10 minutes**, plus cooling

Cooking time **35 minutes**

Serves **4**

200 g (7 oz) **buckwheat flakes**

25 g (1 oz) **sunflower seeds**, toasted

25 g (1 oz) **pumpkin seeds**, toasted

25 g (1 oz) **sesame seeds**, toasted

2 tablespoons **flax seeds**

100 g (3½ oz) **mixed nuts**, roughly chopped

3 tablespoons **runny honey**

2 tablespoons **sunflower oil**

50 g (2 oz) **ready-to-eat dried apricots**, sliced

handful of **dried blueberries**

handful of **dried cranberries**

125 g (4 oz) **fresh blueberries**

125 g (4 oz) **fresh strawberries**, hulled

1 tablespoon **caster sugar**

125 ml (4 fl oz) **natural yogurt**

**Mix** together the buckwheat flakes, all the seeds and the nuts in a large bowl. Gently heat the honey and oil in a small saucepan, then pour into the bowl and stir to coat the mixture.

**Spread** the granola on a baking sheet and cook in a preheated oven, 150°C (300°F), Gas Mark 2, for about 30 minutes.

**Remove** from the oven and break up any large lumps. Place in a large bowl and stir in all the dried fruits. Leave to cool, then store in an airtight container for up to 1–2 weeks.

**Put** the the blueberries, strawberries and sugar in a saucepan with a little water and gently simmer for about 5 minutes until softened. Leave to cool. To serve, spoon the fruit compote in a bowl with the yogurt and sprinkle with the granola.

**For orange & apricot compote**, to serve as an accompaniment alternative, put 200 g (7 oz) ready-to-eat dried apricots, the juice and grated rind of 2 oranges, 1 cinnamon stick, 150 ml (¼ pint) black tea and 2 tablespoons runny honey into a saucepan, and gently simmer for 10 minutes, then leave to cool. Remove the cinnamon stick, place in a food processor or blender and blitz until smooth.

# breakfast cereal bars

Preparation time **10 minutes**
Cooking time **35 minutes**
Makes **16**

100 g (3½ oz) **butter**,
  softened, plus extra
  for greasing
25 g (1 oz) **soft light
  brown sugar**
2 tablespoons **golden syrup**
125 g (4 oz) **millet flakes**
50 g (2 oz) **quinoa**
50 g (2 oz) **dried cherries**
  or **cranberries**
75 g (3 oz) **sultanas**
25 g (1 oz) **sunflower seeds**
25 g (1 oz) **sesame seeds**
25 g (1 oz) **linseeds**
40 g (1½ oz) **unsweetened
  desiccated coconut**
2 **eggs**, lightly beaten

**Grease** a 28 x 20 cm (11 x 8 inch) shallow baking tin.

**Beat** together the butter, sugar and syrup in a large bowl until creamy. Add all the remaining ingredients and beat well until combined.

**Spoon** the mixture into the prepared tin, level the surface with the back of a dessertspoon and place in a preheated oven, 180°C (350°F), Gas Mark 4, for 35 minutes until deep golden. Remove from the oven and leave to cool in the tin.

**Turn** out on to a wooden board and carefully cut into 16 fingers using a serrated knife. Store in an airtight container for up to 5 days.

**For yogurty crunch**, slice 2 bananas and divide half the slices between 4 tall glasses. Mix together 300 ml (½ pint) natural yogurt and 4 tablespoons runny honey in a bowl and spoon half the mixture over the slices. Crumble 4 Breakfast Cereal Bars (see above) and sprinkle half over the yogurt mixture. Repeat the layering, chill and serve.

# french toasts

Preparation time **5 minutes**
Cooking time **5 minutes**
Serves **4**

2 **eggs**, beaten
1 teaspoon **vanilla extract**
100 ml (3½ fl oz) **milk**
1 tablespoon **caster sugar**,
plus extra for sprinkling
½ teaspoon **ground
cinnamon**
4 thick slices of **gluten-free
bread**
25 g (1 oz) **butter**

**Whisk** together the eggs, vanilla extract, milk, sugar and cinnamon in a shallow dish. Place the slices of bread in the mixture, turning to coat both sides so that they absorb the liquid.

**Heat** the butter in a nonstick frying pan. Use a palette knife or a fish slice to remove the soaked bread from the dish and fry the slices for 2 minutes on each side until golden. Cut the toasts in half diagonally into triangles, sprinkle with a little caster sugar and serve.

**For apple & raspberry sauce**, to serve as an accompaniment, heat 25 g (1 oz) butter in a frying pan, add 6 cored and sliced eating apples and fry for 2–3 minutes. Sprinkle over 1 tablespoon soft light brown sugar, ½ teaspoon ground cinnamon and 125 g (4 oz) raspberries and cook gently for 1–2 minutes. Serve over the toasts sprinkled with extra caster sugar.

# mini tomato & feta omelettes

Preparation time **10 minutes**
Cooking time **10 minutes**
Makes **12**

melted **butter**, for greasing
4 **eggs**, beaten
2 tablespoon **chopped chives**
3 **sun-dried tomatoes**,
   finely sliced
75 g (3 oz) **feta cheese**,
   crumbled
**salt** and **black pepper**

**Brush** a 12-hole mini muffin tray lightly with melted butter to grease.

**Mix** together all the remaining ingredients in a large bowl until just combined.

**Pour** the mixture into the greased holes and place in a preheated oven, 220°C (425°F), Gas Mark 7, for about 10 minutes until golden and puffed up. Remove from the oven and serve warm.

**For pea, bacon & Parmesan omelettes**, grill 4 smoked bacon rashers until crisp, then chop. Whisk together the eggs, 2 tablespoons grated Parmesan cheese, 1 tablespoon chopped parsley and 1 tablespoon gluten-free wholegrain mustard in a large bowl. Stir in the bacon and 2 tablespoons peas, thawed if frozen. Pour into the prepared muffin tray and cook as above.

# kedgeree

Preparation time **10 minutes**
Cooking time **20 minutes**
Serves **4**

200 g (7 oz) **basmati rice**
500 g (1 lb) **skinless smoked
  haddock fillets**
2 **bay leaves**
50 g (2 oz) **butter**
1 **onion**, chopped
1 **garlic clove**, crushed
2 tablespoons **curry powder**
4 **spring onions**, finely sliced
handful of **coriander**, chopped
2 **hard-boiled eggs**, roughly
  chopped
**salt and black pepper**

**Cook** the basmati rice in a saucepan of salted boiling water according to the packet instructions. Drain well.

**Place** the haddock in a frying pan with the bay leaves, just cover with water, then simmer for 5–6 minutes until it is just cooked. Drain and flake.

**Heat** the butter in a pan while the haddock is cooking add the onion and garlic and fry for 4–5 minutes until softened. Add the curry powder and continue to fry for 1 minute.

**Stir** in the rice, haddock, spring onions, coriander and eggs. Season well with black pepper and heat through until piping hot. Serve immediately.

**For prawn & pea kedgeree**, omit the haddock and fry the onion and garlic with ½ deseeded and sliced red chilli as above. Add the curry powder and fry for a further minute. Stir in 400 g (13 oz) cooked basmati rice, 300 g (10 oz) cooked peeled prawns, 200 g (7 oz) peas, thawed if frozen, 2 tablespoons chopped mint and the grated rind and juice of ½ lemon. Heat through until piping hot and season well.

# hash breakfast

Preparation time **10 minutes**
Cooking time **10 minutes**
Serves **4**

2 tablespoons **olive oil**
1 **onion**, chopped
500 g (1 lb) cooked **potatoes**, cubed
340 g (11½ oz) can **corned beef**, roughly chopped
dash of **Worcestershire sauce**
4 **eggs**
**black pepper**

**To garnish**
chopped **parsley**
**smoked paprika**

**Heat** half the oil in a large frying pan, add the onion and potatoes and fry for 5–6 minutes or until the potatoes are golden and the onions are softened.

**Stir** in the corned beef and season well with pepper and Worcestershire sauce. Continue to fry for 2–3 minutes.

**Heat** the remaining oil in a frying pan and fry the eggs.

**Spoon** the hash on to 4 serving plates, top each with a fried egg and serve sprinkled with chopped parsley and a little smoked paprika to garnish.

**For breakfast in a pan**, heat all the olive oil in a large frying pan, add 500 g (1 lb) chopped gluten-free sausages and fry for 3–4 minutes until browned and almost cooked through. Add the potatoes and continue to cook for 2–3 minutes until beginning to brown. Stir in a handful of halved cherry tomatoes and 4 sliced spring onions, spread out evenly in the pan, then crack in the eggs and cook for 1–2 minutes. Cut into 4 and serve.

# potato drop scones

Preparation time **10 minutes**
Cooking time **20–25 minutes**
Serves **4**

550 g (1 lb 2 oz) large
  **potatoes**, peeled and cut
  into small chunks
1½ teaspoons **gluten-free
  baking powder**
2 **eggs**
75 ml (3 fl oz) **milk**
**vegetable oil**, for frying
**salt** and **black pepper**

**Cook** the potatoes in a saucepan of salted boiling water for 15 minutes or until tender. Drain well, return to the pan and mash until smooth. Leave to cool slightly.

**Beat** in the baking powder, then the eggs, milk and a little seasoning, and continue to beat until everything is evenly combined.

**Heat** a little oil in a heavy-based frying pan. Drop heaped dessertspoonfuls of the mixture into the pan, spacing them slightly apart, and fry for 3–4 minutes, turning once, until golden. Transfer to a serving plate and keep warm while frying the remainder of the potato mixture.

**Serve** warm, instead of toast, with your favourite cooked breakfast.

**For salmon & potato drop scones**, add 100 g (3½ oz) chopped smoked salmon, 2 tablespoons snipped chives and 3 sliced spring onions to the potato mixture and cook as above.

# yogurt & berry smoothie

Preparation time **5 minutes**
Serves **4**

300 ml (½ pint) **natural yogurt**
500 g (1 lb) fresh or frozen
  **mixed summer berries,**
  thawed if frozen, plus extra
  to decorate
4 tablespoons **millet flakes**
3 tablespoons **runny honey**
300 ml (½ pint) **cranberry**
  **juice**

**Place** all the ingredients in a food processor or a blender and blitz until smooth.

**Pour** into 4 glasses, decorate with a few extra whole berries and serve immediately.

**For frozen raspberry yogurt slice**, blitz 500 g (1 lb) raspberries, 200 g (7 oz) icing sugar, the juice of 1 lemon and 600 ml (1 pint) Greek yogurt in a food processor or blender. Pour the mixture into a 900 g (2 lb) loaf tin that has been lined with clingfilm, then freeze until solid. Serve sliced with mixed berries.

# tropical fruit smoothie

Preparation time **10 minutes**
Serves **4**

1 **mango**, peeled, stoned
  and chopped
2 **kiwifruits**, peeled and
  chopped
1 **banana**, cut into chunks
425 g (14 oz) can **pineapple
  chunks or pieces** in natural
  juice
450 ml (¾ pint) **orange** or
  **apple juice**
handful of **ice cubes**

**Place** all the ingredients in a food processor or blender
and blitz until smooth.

**Pour** into 4 glasses and serve immediately.

**For tropical cocktail**, blitz all the above ingredients
in a food processor or blender with 400ml (14fl oz)
coconut milk and 100 ml (3½ fl oz) white rum. Serve
in 4 glasses over ice.

# lunches & light bites

# tomato & chorizo soup

Preparation time **10 minutes**
Cooking time **25 minutes**
Serves **4**

500 g (1 lb) **red peppers**,
  halved and deseeded
2 tablespoons **olive oil**
1 large **onion**, chopped
2 **garlic cloves**, crushed
150 g (5 oz) **chorizo**
  **sausage**, sliced
1 teaspoon **ground cumin**
1 teaspoon **smoked paprika**
500 g (1 lb) **tomatoes**, halved
  and deseeded
600 ml (1 pint) **gluten-free**
  **chicken** or **vegetable stock**
handful of **parsley**, chopped
**salt** and **black pepper**

**Put** the red peppers on a baking sheet, and drizzle over half the olive oil. Place in a preheated oven 200°C (400°F), Gas Mark 6 for 10–15 minutes, turning after 5 minutes.

**Heat** the remaining olive oil in a large saucepan, while the peppers are roasting, add the onion, garlic and chorizo and fry for 3–4 minutes until the onion is softened and the chorizo is beginning to brown. Stir in the spices and fry for a further minute.

**Add** the tomatoes and the stock to the saucepan and season well. Bring to the boil and simmer for 5 minutes.

**Remove** the red peppers from the oven, skin then roughly chop them and add to the soup and simmer for a further 15 minutes. Remove from the heat and allow to cool for 5 minutes. Roughly blend in a food processor or blender, then stir in the parsley and serve.

**For tomato soup with creamy basil**, omit the red peppers and fry the onion and garlic as above, replacing the chorizo and spices with 1 chopped carrot and 1 chopped celery stick. Add the tomatoes and vegetable stock, bring to the boil and simmer for 25 minutes. Purée in a food processor or blender until smooth. Return to the pan and stir in 2 tablespoons mascarpone cheese and 1 tablespoon pesto. Season and serve.

# thai vegetable, tofu & rice soup

Preparation time **15 minutes**
Cooking time **20 minutes**
Serves **4**

1.2 litres (2 pints) **gluten-free vegetable stock**
2 **lemon grass stalks**, halved and bruised
2 **garlic cloves**, finely sliced
handful of **coriander**, stalks finely chopped and leaves torn
2 **kaffir lime leaves**
2 **red chillies**, deseeded and halved
5 cm (2 inch) **fresh root ginger**, peeled and halved
125 g (4 oz) **fine beans**, topped and tailed, then sliced
225 g (7½ oz) can **water chestnuts**, drained and sliced
200 g (7 oz) **firm tofu**, cubed
150 ml (¼ pint) **coconut cream**
4 **spring onions**, sliced
200 g (7 oz) **basmati rice**, plus extra to serve

**Pour** the stock into a large saucepan, stir in the lemon grass, garlic, coriander stalks, lime leaves, 1 chilli and ginger and simmer for 10 minutes. Remove the pieces of ginger and lemon grass.

**Add** the beans, water chestnuts, tofu and coconut cream and simmer until the beans are just tender. Meanwhile cook the basmati rice in a saucepan of boiling water according to the packet instructions.

**Drain** the rice, then add half the rice to the spring onions and half the basmati rice to the soup and heat through until piping hot.

**Sprinkle** the remaining coriander leaves over the soup, ladle into bowls and garnish with the remaining chilli, finely sliced. Serve with an extra dish of basmati rice for each person.

**For Thai chicken noodle soup**, make the soup as above, replacing the tofu with 300 g (10 oz) cooked and shredded chicken and 1 deseeded and finely sliced red pepper. Omit the rice and replace with 200 g (7 oz) cooked rice noodles.

# sweet potato, squash & coconut soup

Preparation time **10 minutes**
Cooking time **40–45 minutes**
Serves **4**

2 large **sweet potatoes**,
  peeled and cut into chunks
1 large **butternut squash**,
  peeled, deseeded and cut
  into chunks
1 **onion**, cut into wedges
2 **garlic cloves**, peeled
1 teaspoon **cumin seeds**
2 tablespoons **olive oil**
½ teaspoon **dried chilli
  flakes**, plus extra to garnish
  (optional)
900 ml (1½ pints) **gluten-free
  vegetable stock**
200 ml (7 fl oz) **coconut
  cream**
1 teaspoon **garam masala**
**salt** and **black pepper**

**Put** the sweet potatoes, squash, onion and garlic on a baking sheet. Sprinkle over the cumin seeds and drizzle with the oil. Place in a preheated oven, 200°C (400°F), Gas Mark 6, and roast for 25–30 minutes until tender and golden.

**Tip** the roasted vegetables into a large saucepan with the chilli flakes and stock, bring to the boil and simmer for 10 minutes.

**Stir** in the remaining ingredients, heat through until piping hot and then purée in a food processor or blender until smooth. Serve, garnished with a pinch of chilli flakes, and with toasted gluten-free bread.

**For squash & lentil soup**, roast the squash, onion and garlic as above, omitting the sweet potatoes, for 20 minutes. Transfer to a large saucepan and, when nearly cooked, add 100 g (3½ oz) split red lentils (rinsed and drained) and 1.2 litres (2 pints) gluten-free vegetable stock. Bring to the boil and simmer for about 25 minutes until the lentils and squash are soft. Purée in a food processor or blender until smooth and season well. Serve with warm crusty gluten-free bread.

# mexican bean soup

Preparation time **10 minutes**
Cooking time **30 minutes**
Serves **4**

1 tablespoon **olive oil**
1 **onion**, chopped
1 **garlic clove**, crushed
1 **red chilli**, deseeded
  and chopped
bunch of **coriander**, stalks and
  leaves chopped separately
1 **green pepper**, cored,
  deseeded and chopped
1 teaspoon **ground cumin**
1 teaspoon **smoked paprika**
2 x 400 g (13 oz) cans **black-
  eyed beans**, drained
  and rinsed
400 g (13 oz) can **chopped
  tomatoes**
2 tablespoons **sun-dried
  tomato paste**
600 ml (1 pint) **gluten-free
  vegetable stock**
**salt** and **black pepper**

**Heat** the oil in a large saucepan, add the onion, garlic and chilli and fry for 2 minutes. Add the coriander stalks and green pepper and continue to fry for 2–3 minutes, then stir in the cumin and paprika.

**Stir** in the beans, tomatoes, tomato paste and stock, bring to the boil and simmer for 20 minutes.

**Purée** half the soup in a food processor or blender, then return to the pan with the coriander leaves (reserving 4 for garnish), season well and heat through until piping hot. Serve garnished with the reserved coriander leaves.

**For guacamole**, to serve as an accompaniment, roughly mash 1 stoned and peeled large ripe avocado with the juice of 1 lime in a bowl. Stir in 4 sliced spring onions, a handful of chopped coriander, 1 small deseeded and chopped red chilli and a good seasoning of salt. Add a spoonful of the guacamole to the soup before serving.

# fish chowder

Preparation time **10 minutes**
Cooking time **30 minutes**
Serves **4**

15 g (½ oz) **butter**
1 tablespoon **vegetable oil**
1 **onion**, finely chopped
100 g (3½ oz) **streaky bacon**,
  chopped
2 tablespoons **cornflour**
600 ml (1 pint) **gluten-free
  fish stock**
600 ml (1 pint) **milk**
500 g (1 lb) **floury potatoes**,
  peeled and cubed
500 g (1 lb) mixed **skinless
  firm white fish fillets**, cubed
300 g (10 oz) **skinless
  smoked haddock fillets**,
  cubed
250 g (8 oz) **raw prawns**,
  peeled and deveined
150 ml (¼ pint) **single cream**
**salt** and **black pepper**
chopped **parsley**, to garnish

**Heat** the butter and oil in a large saucepan, add the onion and fry for 3 minutes until softened. Add the bacon and fry for a further 3–4 minutes until beginning to brown.

**Add** in the cornflour and cook, stirring, for 1 minute, then gradually add the stock and milk and cook, stirring all the time, until thickened and smooth. Mix in the potatoes and simmer for 10 minutes, then add the fish and cook gently for a further 5–6 minutes until just cooked through.

**Mix** in the prawns and cream and cook until the prawns are cooked through and piping hot. Season well, ladle into bowls and serve sprinkled with the parsley.

**For spiced corn chowder**, fry the onion as above, adding 1 deseeded and chopped red chilli. Omit the bacon. Stir in the cornflour and then gradually stir in 600 ml (1 pint) gluten-free vegetable stock and the milk as above. Mix in 600 g (1 ¼ lb) peeled and chopped potatoes and 2 x 200 g (7 oz) cans of sweetcorn, drained and simmer until the potato is tender. Season well, ladle into bowls and sprinkle over a handful of chopped parsley or coriander.

# chicken & ham soup

Preparation time **20 minutes**
Cooking time **1 hour**
**20 minutes**
Serves **8**

375 g (12 oz) piece of
**lean gammon**
3 tablespoons **olive oil**
4 large **skinless chicken**
**thighs**
3 **onions**, chopped
2 **celery sticks**, sliced
2 **bay leaves**
600 ml (1 pint) **gluten-free**
**chicken stock**
375 g (12 oz) **potatoes**,
peeled and cut into
small dice
150 g (5 oz) **frozen**
**sweetcorn**

**Dumplings**
125 g (4 oz) **fine cornmeal**
100 g (3½ oz) **gluten-free**
**flour**
2 teaspoons **gluten-free**
**baking powder**
1 tablespoon chopped **thyme**
40 g (1½ oz) chilled **butter**
**salt** and **black pepper**

**Chop** the gammon into 1 cm (½ inch) chunks. Heat the oil in a large heavy-based saucepan, add the chicken, onions and celery and fry gently for 10 minutes, stirring until golden.

**Add** the gammon, bay leaves, stock and 600 ml (1 pint) water and bring to the boil. Reduce the heat, cover and simmer gently for 40 minutes until the chicken and ham are tender.

**Lift** out the chicken with a slotted spoon and, when cool enough to handle, shred the flesh from the bones. Return the flesh to the pan with the potatoes and sweetcorn. Simmer, covered, for 20 minutes, until the potatoes are tender.

**Make** the dumplings. Mix together the cornmeal, flour, baking powder, thyme and seasoning in a bowl until evenly combined. Grate the butter into the mixture and add 250 ml (8 fl oz) water. Mix to a thick paste, adding a little more water if necessary.

**Use** 2 dessertspoons to roughly pat the paste into 8 rounds and spoon into the soup. Cover and simmer gently for about 10 minutes until the dumplings are light and puffy.

**For pea & ham soup**, place 150 g (5 oz) rinsed and drained yellow split peas, 1 litre (1¾ pints) water, 75 g (3 oz) chopped smoked ham, 1 large chopped carrot, 1 chopped onion and 2 bay leaves into a large saucepan, bring to the boil, removing any scum that comes to the surface, cover and simmer for 40 minutes until the split peas are tender. Purée in a food processor or blender, season well and serve sprinkled with chopped parsley.

# chilled gazpacho

Preparation time **20 minutes**, plus chilling
Serves **6**

875 g (1¾ lb) **tomatoes**, skinned and roughly chopped
½ **cucumber**, roughly chopped
2 **red peppers**, cored, deseeded and roughly chopped
1 **celery stick**, chopped
2 **garlic cloves**, chopped
½ **red chilli**, deseeded and sliced
small handful of **coriander**
2 tablespoons **white wine vinegar**
2 tablespoons **sun-dried tomato paste**
4 tablespoons **olive oil**
**salt**
**ice cubes**, to serve

**Mix** together the vegetables, garlic, chilli and coriander in a large bowl. Add the vinegar, tomato paste, oil and a little salt.

**Blitz** in batches in a food processor or blender until smooth, scraping the mixture down from the side of the bowl if necessary.

**Collect** the blended mixtures together in a clean bowl and check the seasoning, adding a little more salt if needed. Cover and chill for up to 24 hours.

**When** ready to serve, ladle the gazpacho into large bowls and scatter with ice cubes.

**For gazpacho topping**, to serve as an accompaniment, heat 2 tablespoons olive oil in a frying pan, add 150 g (5 oz) gluten-free bread cubes and fry until golden. Place the croutons in a bowl and stir in 2 sliced spring onions, 1 cored, deseeded and finely sliced green pepper, 2 roughly chopped hard-boiled eggs and a handful of chopped coriander. Sprinkle over the gazpacho before serving.

# chickpea & feta salad

Preparation time **10 minutes**
Cooking time **10–15 minutes**
Serves **4**

500 g (1 lb) **red peppers**,
  halved and deseeded
4 tablespoons **olive oil**
2 x 400 g (13 oz) cans
  **chickpeas**, drained
  and rinsed
150 g (5 oz) **feta cheese**,
  crumbled
1 **red chilli**, deseeded and
  finely sliced
75 g (3 oz) **rocket leaves** or
  **baby leaf spinach**
125 g (4 oz) **cherry tomatoes**,
  quartered
handful of **mint**, chopped
handful of **coriander**, chopped
drizzle of **red wine vinegar**
**black pepper**

**Put** the red peppers on a baking sheet, drizzle over half the olive oil and place in a preheated oven, 200°C (400°F), Gas Mark 6, for 10–15 minutes, turning after 5 minutes. Peel off the skins and slice the flesh.

**Remove** from the oven and place in a large serving bowl. Add the chickpeas, feta, chilli, rocket leaves or spinach, tomatoes and herbs to the serving bowl and mix together with a large spoon.

**Drizzle** the remaining olive oil over the salad, add the red wine vinegar, season with pepper and gently mix.

**Serve** the salad with grilled meats or fish, or with a gluten-free warmed pitta bread.

**For lentil & tomato salad with crispy bacon**, cook 250 g (8 oz) Puy lentils in a saucepan of boiling water according to the packet instructions then drain well. Whisk together 2 tablespoons olive oil, 2 teaspoons gluten-free Dijon mustard, 2 teaspoons runny honey, 1 tablespoon balsamic vinegar and a handful of chopped fresh herbs in a bowl. Stir in the warm lentils with 2 large handfuls of baby leaf spinach, 75 g (3 oz) semi-dried tomatoes and 100 g (3½ oz) crumbled soft goats' cheese. Grill 6 smoked streaky bacon rashers until brown and crisp, cool a little, then roughly chop and scatter over the salad.

# potato & avocado salad

Preparation time **10 minutes**
Cooking time **12–15 minutes**
Serves **4**

600 g (1 ¼ lb) small **new
    potatoes**
1 ripe **avocado**
1 punnet **mustard and cress**
grated rind of ½ **lemon**
75 g (3 oz) **rocket leaves**
**salt** and **black pepper**

**Dressing**
1 tablespoon **gluten-free
    wholegrain mustard**
juice of ½ **lemon**
2 tablespoons **mayonnaise**

**Cook** the potatoes in a saucepan of salted boiling water for 12–15 minutes or until just tender.

**Drain** well and place in a large salad bowl.

**Halve** the avocado and remove the stone. Cut the flesh into pieces. Whisk together the dressing ingredients in a small bowl, then add to the warm potatoes. Mix in the avocado pieces, mustard and cress, lemon rind and rocket. Season well.

**Divide** the salad between 4 plates and serve.

**For potato & sun-dried tomato salad**, cook the potatoes as above, drain well and place in a large salad bowl. While they are still warm, stir in 6 sliced, drained sun-dried tomatoes in oil, 12 sliced pitted olives, 2 tablespoons pesto and 3 tablespoons light crème fraîche. Season with plenty of black pepper.

# roasted veggie & quinoa salad

Preparation time **5 minutes**
Cooking time **20–25 minutes**
Serves **4**

3 **courgettes**, cut into chunks
2 **red peppers**, cored,
 deseeded and cut into
 chunks
2 **red onions**, cut into wedges
1 large **aubergine**, cut into
 chunks
3 **garlic cloves**, peeled
3 tablespoons **olive oil**
150 g (5 oz) **quinoa**
2 tablespoons **green pesto** or
 **sun-dried tomato paste**
1 tablespoon **balsamic**
 **vinegar**
75 g (3 oz) **rocket leaves**

**Put** all the vegetables and garlic on a large baking sheet and drizzle over the olive oil. Place in a preheated oven, 220°C (425°F), Gas Mark 7, for 20–25 minutes until tender and beginning to char.

**Cook** the quinoa, meanwhile, in a saucepan of boiling water according to the pack instructions, then drain well.

**Whisk** together the pesto or tomato paste and balsamic vinegar in a small bowl. Place the roasted vegetables, rocket and quinoa in a large serving bowl and stir in the dressing. Serve warm.

**For quinoa with salmon & watercress**, cook the quinoa as above. Meanwhile, place 2 large pieces of skinless salmon fillet, about 300 g (10 oz) total weight, in a nonstick frying pan and cook for 3 minutes on each side until crisp and just cooked through, then flake. Whisk together 200 g (7 oz) light crème fraîche, the grated rind and juice of 1 orange and 1 tablespoon gluten-free wholegrain mustard in a small bowl. Stir the dressing into the quinoa with the flaked salmon and a bunch of chopped watercress.

# italian bread salad

Preparation time **10 minutes**,
  plus standing
Cooking time **10 minutes**
Serves **4**

2 **red peppers**, deseeded
  and sliced
3 tablespoons **olive oil**
650 g (1 lb 5 oz) **tomatoes**,
  skinned, cored and chopped
1 **red onion**, finely sliced
handful of **green olives**
1 tablespoon **capers**, rinsed
1 **red chilli**, deseeded and
  finely chopped
handful of **basil leaves**
2 tablespoons **red wine
  vinegar**
4 tablespoons **olive oil**
200 g (7 oz) **gluten-free
  bread**, cubed and toasted
**salt** and **black pepper**

**Put** the red peppers on a baking sheet, drizzle over
half the olive oil and place in a preheated oven 200°C
(400°F), Gas Mark 6 for 10 minutes, turning after
5 minutes. Leave to cool then remove the skin.

**Leave** to cool. Mix together all the remaining ingredients,
apart from the toasted bread cubes, in a large bowl and
set aside for at least 20 minutes to allow the flavours
to develop.

**Add** the red peppers to the bowl when cooled. Just
before serving, add the toasted bread cubes, stir, then
serve with grilled meats.

### For Mediterranean vegetable & chicken pasta,
omit the bread from the above recipe and replace
with 375 g (12 oz) gluten-free pasta shapes cooked
in a saucepan of salted boiling water according to the
pack instructions. Mix together with the remaining
ingredients, reserving 1 tablespoon of the oil.
Meanwhile, mix together 1 crushed garlic clove, the
reserved oil, 1 tablespoon thyme leaves and 1 teaspoon
balsamic vinegar and pour over 4 sliced boneless,
skinless chicken breasts in a dish. Cover and leave to
marinate for 10 minutes. Drain the pasta well, put in a
large bowl and mix with the roasted peppers and all the
other ingredients as above but only using 3 tablespoons
of the olive oil. Heat a griddle pan until hot and cook
the chicken for 2–3 minutes on each side until cooked
through, then serve on top of the vegetable pasta.

# walnut, pear & green leaf salad

Preparation time **10 minutes**
Cooking time **2–3 minutes**
Serves **4**

**vegetable oil**, for oiling
75 g (3 oz) **Parmesan cheese**, grated
2 large **ripe pears**
50 g (2 oz) **walnut pieces**, lightly toasted
125 g (4 oz) **mixed leaves salad**

**Dressing**
6 tablespoons **walnut oil**
2 tablespoons **lemon juice**
1 tablespoon **gluten-free grainy mustard**
2 teaspoons **caster sugar**
several **tarragon** sprigs, roughly chopped
**salt** and **black pepper**

**Oil** a foil-lined baking sheet and scatter the Parmesan over it, spreading it into a thin layer about 25 cm (10 inches) square. Cook under a hot grill for 2–3 minutes until the cheese has melted and is pale golden in colour. Leave until cool enough to handle, then peel the foil away, letting the cheese break into pieces to form 'croutes'.

**Whisk** together the dressing ingredients in a large bowl. Halve and core the pears then cut into thin slices.

**Add** the pears, walnuts and salad leaves to the bowl with the dressing and toss together. Pile on to 4 serving plates and scatter with the Parmesan croutes.

**For blue cheese & pear salad**, whisk together 1 tablespoon sweet chilli sauce, 1 tablespoon olive oil and 1 tablespoon red wine vinegar in a small bowl. Mix together 100 g (3½ oz) rocket leaves, 2 sliced heads of chicory, 1 pear, cored and sliced, 100 g (3½ oz) walnut pieces and 125 g (4 oz) crumbled blue cheese in a large serving bowl, drizzle over the dressing and serve.

# goats' cheese & onion tarts

Preparation time **15 minutes**, plus chilling
Cooking time **12–15 minutes**
Serves **4**

100 g (3½ oz) **rice flour**, plus extra for dusting
1 tablespoon **polenta**
75 g (3 oz) **butter**, cubed
1 tablespoon grated **Parmesan cheese**
1 **egg yolk**

**Filling**
2 tablespoons **onion marmalade** or **chutney**
75 g (3 oz) **soft goats' cheese**, crumbled
1 teaspoon **thyme leaves**

**Place** the rice flour, polenta, butter and Parmesan in a food processor and whizz until the mixture resembles fine breadcrumbs. Alternatively, mix together the rice flour and polenta in a bowl. Add the butter and rub in with the fingertips until the mix resembles fine breadcrumbs. Stir in the Parmesan.

**Add** the egg yolk and enough cold water to form a soft but not sticky dough. Wrap in clingfilm and chill for 30 minutes.

**Roll** the dough out on a surface lightly dusted with rice flour and use a 10 cm (4 inch) plain cutter to stamp out 4 rounds, rerolling the trimmings as necessary.

**Put** the pastry rounds on a baking sheet lightly dusted with rice flour, then spoon over the onion marmalade or chutney, dot with the goats' cheese and sprinkle over the thyme.

**Place** in a preheated oven, 200°C (400°F), Gas Mark 6, for 12–15 minutes until golden. Serve with a spinach and rocket leaf salad, if liked.

**For Mediterranean tarts**, make the pastry as above and spoon 1 teaspoon sun-dried tomato paste over the pastry rounds. Grill, skin, deseed and slice 1 red pepper, then mix together with 12 black olives, 100 g (3½ oz) crumbled feta cheese and 3 drained and sliced bottled artichoke hearts. Divide between the pastries, then bake as above.

# crab cakes

Preparation time **15 minutes**, plus chilling
Cooking time **20 minutes**
Serves **4**

300 g (10 oz) **potatoes**, peeled and chopped
375 g (12 oz) **fresh white crab meat**
3 **spring onions**, sliced
handful of **coriander**, leaves and stalks finely chopped
good squeeze of **lime juice**
½ **chilli**, deseeded and finely chopped
1 **egg yolk**
3 tablespoons **polenta**
2 tablespoons **vegetable oil**
**salt** and **black pepper**

**To serve**
**lime wedges**
**mixed leaf salad**

**Cook** the potatoes in a saucepan of salted boiling water for 15 minutes or until tender. Drain well, return to the pan and mash. Leave to cool. Stir in all the remaining ingredients except the polenta and oil.

**Put** the polenta on a plate, shape the crab mixture into 8 cakes and coat in the polenta. Cover and chill for 20 minutes.

**Heat** the oil in a large frying pan, add the cakes and fry for 2–3 minutes on each side until golden. Serve with lime wedges and a mixed leaf salad.

**For chilli dipping sauce**, to serve as an accompaniment, place 75 g (3 oz) caster sugar and 4 tablespoons water in a saucepan, heat until the sugar has dissolved, then bubble until it turns a caramel colour. Stir in 2 deseeded and chopped red chillies, 1 sliced lemon grass stalk, 1 sliced garlic clove, the grated rind and juice of 1 lime and 1 tablespoon peeled and finely shredded fresh root ginger. Pour into a serving dish and leave to cool.

# sweet potatoes with tomato salsa

Preparation time **5 minutes**
Cooking time **45 minutes**
Serves **4**

4 large **sweet potatoes**, about
   275 g (9 oz) each
2 tablespoons **olive oil**
100 g (3½ oz) **Emmental** or
   **Cheddar cheese**, grated
**salt**

**Salsa**
4 large **tomatoes**
1 small **red onion**, finely
   chopped
2 **celery sticks**, finely chopped
handful of **coriander**, chopped
4 tablespoons **lime juice**
4 teaspoons **caster sugar**

**Scrub** the potatoes and put them in a small roasting tin.
Prick with a fork, drizzle with the oil and sprinkle with a
little salt. Place in a preheated oven, 200°C (400°F),
Gas Mark 6, for 45 minutes until tender.

**Make** the salsa, meanwhile. Finely chop the tomatoes
and mix with the onion, celery, coriander, lime juice and
sugar in a bowl.

**Halve** the potatoes and fluff up the flesh with a fork.
Sprinkle with the cheese and top with the salsa. Serve
with a green salad.

**For baked sweet potatoes with citrus spiced butter**,
cook the sweet potatoes as above. Meanwhile, beat
together 50 g (2 oz) softened butter, ½ teaspoon dried
chilli flakes, the grated rind of 1 orange and 2 tablespoons
chopped coriander in a small bowl. Spoon on to the halved
baked potatoes and serve with griddled chicken, if liked.

# quick nachos

Preparation time **5 minutes**
Cooking time **1–2 minutes**
Serves **4**

200 g (7 oz) **gluten-free plain corn tortilla chips**
300 g (10 oz) **ready-made fresh tomato salsa**
125 g (4 oz) **Monterey Jack** or **Cheddar cheese**, grated
handful of **coriander,** chopped
**soured cream**, to serve

**Put** the tortilla chips into a wide ovenproof dish. Spoon over the tomato salsa, then sprinkle over the grated cheese and coriander.

**Place** under a medium grill and cook for 1–2 minutes until the cheese is golden and bubbling. Serve with soured cream.

**For chilli beef nachos**, heat 1 tablespoon olive oil in a frying pan, add 1 chopped onion, 1 crushed garlic clove and 1 deseeded and sliced red chilli and fry for 2–3 minutes. Add 300 g (10 oz) lean minced beef and fry for 2–3 minutes until browned. Stir in the tomato salsa as above and a 400 g (13 oz) can drained kidney beans and simmer for 20 minutes. Spoon the mixture over the tortilla chips in an ovenproof dish, scatter over the cheese, then place under the grill as above.

# spinach, tomato & parmesan scones

Preparation time **10 minutes**
Cooking time **12–15 minutes**
Makes **8**

175 g (6 oz) **rice flour**, plus
extra for dusting
75 g (3 oz) **cornflour**
1 teaspoon **gluten-free
baking powder**
1 teaspoon **bicarbonate
of soda**
75 g (3 oz) **butter**, cubed
100 g (3½ oz) **frozen leaf
spinach**, thawed, squeezed
of any liquid and chopped
4 **sun-dried tomatoes in oil**,
drained and finely chopped
50 g (2 oz) **Parmesan
cheese**, grated
good grating of **nutmeg**
1 large **egg**, beaten
3 tablespoons **buttermilk**, plus
extra for brushing

**Place** the rice flour, cornflour, baking powder, bicarbonate of soda and butter in a food processor and whizz until the mixture resembles fine breadcrumbs. Alternatively, mix together the dry ingredients in a large bowl. Add the butter and rub in with the fingertips until the mixture resembles fine breadcrumbs. Mix in the spinach, sun-dried tomatoes, Parmesan and nutmeg.

**Whisk** together the egg and buttermilk with a fork in a separate bowl, stir in the flour mixture and combine to form a soft dough.

**Turn** the dough out on a surface lightly dusted with rice flour, press out to a thickness of 2.5 cm (1 inch) and use a 5 cm (2 inch) cutter to stamp out 8 scones, rerolling the trimmings as necessary.

**Put** on a baking sheet lightly dusted with rice flour, brush with a little buttermilk and place in a preheated oven, 220°C (425°F), Gas Mark 7, for 12–15 minutes until risen and golden. Serve warm, spread with butter or to accompany the soup.

**For olive, feta & herb scones**, make the dough as above, omitting the spinach, sun-dried tomatoes and nutmeg and replacing with 18 sliced pitted olives, 100 g (3½ oz) crumbled feta cheese and 1 tablespoon chopped fresh herbs. Continue as above.

# courgette, beetroot & feta fritters

Preparation time **10 minutes**
Cooking time **6–12 minutes**
Serves **4**

1 large **courgette**, grated
grated rind of **1 lemon**
2 **spring onions**, sliced
2 tablespoons chopped
  **parsley**
2 tablespoons chopped **mint**
100 g (3½ oz) **feta cheese**,
  crumbled
2 tablespoons **rice flour**
1 **egg yolk**
2 cooked **beetroot**, peeled
  and grated
2 tablespoons **olive oil**
**salt** and **black pepper**
**basil leaves**, to garnish
**mixed leaf salad**, to serve

**Mix** together the courgette, lemon rind, spring onions, herbs, feta, rice flour and egg yolk in a large bowl and season well. Gently stir in the beetroot until the mixture is just speckled with red.

**Heat** a little of the oil in a frying pan, add tablespoons of the mixture to the pan and fry the fritters for 1–2 minutes on each side until golden. Transfer to a serving plate and keep warm while frying the remainder of the mixture, adding the remaining oil to the pan as necessary.

**Garnish** the fritters with basil leaves and a mixed leaf salad.

**For cucmber & yogurt dip**, to serve as an accompaniment, mix together 200 ml (7 fl oz) Greek yogurt, 1 crushed garlic clove, 1 teaspoon toasted cumin seeds, ¼ grated cucumber, squeezed of excess liquid, and a pinch of paprika in a serving dish. Season well.

# sushi triangles

Preparation time **20 minutes**
Serves **4**

400 g (13 oz) cooked
  **sushi rice**
**sushi rice seasoning**, to taste
4 sheets of **nori seaweed**
100 g (3½ oz) **smoked
  salmon**
50 g (2 oz) **cucumber**, very
  thinly sliced

**To serve**
**gluten-free soy sauce**
**wasabi**

**Season** the rice to taste with the sushi rice seasoning.

**Place** 2 of the seaweed sheets on to a board. Spread a quarter of the rice over each, cover with the smoked salmon, then the cucumber. Spoon over the remaining rice, then top with the other seaweed sheets. Press the sushi down well so the layers stick together.

**Cut** into 4 triangles and serve with soy and wasabi.

**For prawn & roasted pepper sushi**, season the rice as above, then layer onto the seaweed sheets with 100 g (3½ oz) cooked peeled prawns, 1 sliced roasted red pepper and 1 stoned, peeled and sliced ripe avocado. Top with the remaining seaweed sheets and continue as above.

# gruyère & olive drop scones

Preparation time **10 minutes**
Cooking time **6–12 minutes**
Serves **4**

250 g (8 oz) **ricotta cheese**
150 ml (¼ pint) **milk**
3 **eggs**, separated
100 g (3½ oz) **rice flour**
1 teaspoon **gluten-free baking powder**
1 tablespoon chopped **chives**
12 **pitted olives**, quartered
50 g (2 oz) **Gruyère cheese**, grated
2 tablespoons grated **Parmesan cheese**
15 g (½ oz) **butter**

**To serve (optional)**
**grilled bacon rashers**
**cherry tomatoes**, halved

**Beat** together the ricotta, milk and egg yolks in a large bowl. Sift together the flour and baking powder in a separate bowl, then fold into the ricotta mixture.

**Whisk** the egg whites in a clean bowl until they form stiff peaks, then fold into the ricotta mixture with the chives, olives, Gruyère and Parmesan.

**Heat** a little of the butter in a nonstick frying pan, add spoonfuls of the mixture and fry for 1–2 minutes on each side. Transfer to a serving plate and keep warm while frying the remainder of the mixture, adding the remaining butter to the pan as necessary.

**Serve** warm with crispy grilled bacon and halved cherry tomatoes, if liked.

**For pear & cinnamon drop scones**, make the drop scone mixture as above, omitting the chives, olives and cheeses. Peel, core and roughly chop 2 ripe pears and stir into the mixture with 2 tablespoons caster sugar and 1 teaspoon ground cinnamon. Cook as above. Serve with a drizzle of honey and a spoonful of light crème fraîche.

# butterbean & chorizo stew

Preparation time **10 minutes**
Cooking time **20 minutes**
Serves **4**

1 tablespoon **olive oil**
1 large **onion**, chopped
2 **garlic cloves**, crushed
200 g (7 oz) **chorizo
  sausage**, sliced
1 **green pepper**, cored,
  deseeded and chopped
1 **red pepper**, cored,
  deseeded and chopped
1 glass **red wine**
2 x 400 g (13 oz) cans
  **butterbeans**, drained
  and rinsed
400 g (13 oz) can **cherry
  tomatoes**
1 tablespoon **tomato purée**
**salt** and **black pepper**
chopped **parsley**, to garnish
**gluten-free crusty bread**,
  to serve

**Heat** the oil in a flameproof casserole, add the onion and garlic and fry for 1–2 minutes. Stir in the chorizo and fry until beginning to brown. Add the peppers and fry for 3 minutes.

**Pour** in the wine and allow to bubble, then stir in the butterbeans, tomatoes and tomato purée and season well. Cover and simmer for 15 minutes. Ladle into shallow bowls, sprinkle with the parsley to garnish and serve with crusty gluten-free bread.

**For garlic prawns with butterbeans**, cook the onion and garlic as above, then stir in 300 g (10 oz) raw peeled and deveined tiger prawns instead of the chorizo and fry until they just turn pink. Add the butterbeans, 3 tablespoons light crème fraîche and 2 handfuls of rocket leaves and season well. Heat through and serve.

# cheesy cauliflower & broccoli bake

Preparation time **10 minutes**
Cooking time **20 minutes**
Serves 4

50 g (2 oz) **butter**
1 **cauliflower**, cut into florets
1 head of **broccoli**, cut into
  florets
25 g (1 oz) **cornflour**
300 ml (½ pint) **milk**
100 g (3½ oz) **Gruyère
  cheese**, grated
8 **streaky bacon rashers**,
  grilled until crisp
50 g (2 oz) **gluten-free fresh
  breadcrumbs**
**salt** and **black pepper**

**Heat** half the butter in a frying pan, add the cauliflower
and broccoli and fry until just tender. Transfer to an
ovenproof dish.

**Melt** the remaining butter in a saucepan, add the
cornflour and cook, stirring, for 1 minute. Gradually add
the milk and cook, stirring all the time, until thickened
and smooth, then season well. Stir in two-thirds of the
Gruyère, then crumble in half the bacon.

**Pour** the sauce over the vegetables. Mix together the
remaining Gruyère and the breadcrumbs and sprinkle
over the top with the remaining bacon.

**Place** in a preheated oven, 200°C (400°F), Gas Mark 6,
for 10–12 minutes until golden and bubbling.

**For leek & Jerusalem artichoke gratin**, replace
the cauliflower and broccoli with 3 finely sliced large
leeks and 300 g (10 oz) peeled and sliced Jerusalem
artichokes and cook as above until softened. Spoon
into an ovenproof dish. Mix together 100 g (3½ oz)
gluten-free fresh breadcrumbs, 50 g (2 oz) crumbled
feta cheese and 50 g (2 oz) grated Gruyère cheese in
a bowl, sprinkle over the leek mixture and press down
gently. Cook in the oven as above.

# rice & sweetcorn omelette

Preparation time **5 minutes**
Cooking time **10 minutes**
Serves **4**

15 g (½ oz) **butter**
4 **spring onions**, shredded
1 **red chilli**, deseeded and
  finely sliced (optional)
200 g (7 oz) can **sweetcorn**,
  drained
200 g (7 oz) cooked **long-
  grain** or **basmati rice**
handful of **fresh herbs**,
  chopped
6 **eggs**, beaten
3 tablespoons grated
  **Parmesan cheese**
**salt** and **black pepper**

**Heat** the butter in a large frying pan, add the spring onions and chilli and fry for 2 minutes. Add the sweetcorn, rice and herbs and stir to combine.

**Pour** in the eggs, season well and cook for 2–3 minutes until beginning to set.

**Sprinkle** over the Parmesan, then place under a hot grill and cook until firm and golden. Turn out and cut into generous wedges to serve.

**For chorizo & potato omelette**, heat 1 tablespoon olive oil in a frying pan, add 1 sliced onion and fry for 3–4 minutes until softened. Add 125 g (4 oz) chopped chorizo sausage and fry for a further 2 minutes until it begins to crisp. Stir in 300 g (10 oz) cooked sliced potatoes and a handful of chopped parsley. Stir to combine, then pour in the beaten eggs. Cook under a hot grill as above.

# ricotta & spinach tart

Preparation time **15 minutes**, plus chilling

Cooking time **30 minutes**

Serves **4**

150 g (5 oz) **rice flour**, plus extra for dusting

100 g (3½ oz) **polenta**

125 g (4 oz) **butter**, cubed

25 g (1 oz) **Parmesan cheese**, grated

1 **egg yolk**

2 tablespoons **milk**

**Filling**

1 teaspoon **olive oil**

1 **shallot**, finely chopped

1 **garlic clove**, crushed

175 g (6 oz) **baby leaf spinach**

300 g (10 oz) **ricotta cheese**

100 g (3½ oz) **light crème fraîche**

4 tablespoons grated **Parmesan cheese**

2 **eggs**, lightly beaten

grating of **nutmeg**

**salt** and **black pepper**

**Place** the flour, polenta, butter and Parmesan in a food processor and whizz until the mixture resembles fine breadcrumbs. Alternatively, mix together the rice flour and polenta in a bowl. Add the butter and rub in with fingertips until the mixture resembles fine breadcrumbs. Stir in the Parmesan.

**Mix** together the egg yolk and milk in a separate bowl and add enough to the dry ingredients to form a soft but not sticky dough. Wrap the dough in clingfilm and chill for 30 minutes. Roll the dough out on a surface lightly dusted with rice flour and use to line a 20 cm (8 inch) fluted tart tin. Prick the pastry base with a fork and place in a preheated oven, 200°C (400°F), Gas Mark 6, for 10 minutes. Remove from the oven.

**Make** the filling while the pastry is cooking. Heat the oil in a frying pan and soften the shallot and garlic for 2–3 minutes. Add the spinach and cook for 3–4 minutes until wilted and any moisture has evaporated.

**Beat** together the ricotta, crème fraîche, half the Parmesan and the eggs in a bowl, then season well with nutmeg and salt and pepper. Stir in the spinach and pour into the tart case, sprinkle over the remaining Parmesan and return to the oven for 20 minutes until firm and golden.

**For creamy smoked trout tart,** make and bake the tart case as above. For the filling, beat together 2 eggs, 100 g (3½ oz) cream cheese, 200 ml (7 fl oz) light crème fraîche, 1 tablespoon creamed horseradish and 2 tablespoons snipped chives in a bowl. Fold in 150 g (5 oz) sliced smoked trout, pour into the tart case and cook in the oven for 20–25 minutes until firm and golden.

# vietnamese rice paper rolls

Preparation time **15 minutes**
Makes **12**

125 g (4 oz) **cooked peeled prawns**
¼ **cucumber**, cut into matchsticks
handful of **coriander**, chopped
handful of **mint**, chopped
handful of **Thai basil**, chopped
150 g (5 oz) cold cooked **rice vermicelli**
¼ **iceberg lettuce**, shredded
12 **round rice paper sheets**
**lime wedges**, to serve

**Dipping sauce**
2 tablespoons **sweet chilli dipping sauce**
juice of 1 **lime**
1 tablespoon **Thai fish sauce**
1 tablespoon **sesame seeds**, toasted

**Mix** together the prawns, cucumber, herbs, vermicelli and lettuce in a large bowl.

**Soak** 1 rice sheet in a bowl of warm water for 20 seconds, then drain on kitchen paper. Fill with the prawn mixture, leaving about 2.5 cm (1 inch) at the top and the bottom of the sheet. Fold over the top and bottom edges and roll up. Repeat with the remaining rice sheets and filling.

**Whisk** together all the dipping sauce ingredients in a serving dish and serve with the rolls and lime wedges.

**For crab rolls**, omit the prawns and cucumber and replace with 200 g (7 oz) fresh white crab meat and 4 finely sliced spring onions. Continue as above. Serve with chopped peanuts, if liked.

# double-baked cheese soufflés

Preparation time **15 minutes**
Cooking time **30–40 minutes**
Serves **4**

25 g (1 oz) **butter**, plus extra, melted, for greasing
25 g (1 oz) **rice flour**
225 ml (7½ fl oz) **milk**
75 g (3 oz) **blue cheese**, crumbled
75 g (3 oz) **Parmesan cheese**, grated
1 teaspoon **gluten-free English mustard**
1 tablespoon **snipped chives**
1 tablespoon **thyme leaves**
2 **eggs**, separated
100 ml (3½ fl oz) **double cream**
**salt** and **black pepper**

**Brush** 4 small ramekins with melted butter to grease.

**Heat** the butter in a saucepan, add the flour and cook, stirring, for 1 minute. Gradually add the milk and cook, stirring all the time, until thickened and smooth. Remove from the heat and cool a little. Stir in the blue cheese, half the Parmesan, the mustard, herbs and egg yolks and season well.

**Whisk** the egg whites in a clean bowl until they form soft peaks, then gently fold into the cheese sauce. Spoon into the prepared ramekins, then place in a roasting tin. Pour boiling water into the tin to come halfway up the ramekins and then place in a preheated oven, 180°C (350°F), Gas Mark 4, for 15–20 minutes until firm. Cool completely.

**Mix** together the cream and the remaining Parmesan when ready to serve and spoon over the soufflés. Place in a preheated oven, 220°C (425°F), Gas Mark 7, for 10–15 minutes or until golden and risen. Serve with a watercress salad.

**For blue cheese soufflé omelette for one**, separate 3 large eggs and whisk the whites in a large clean bowl until they form soft peaks. Gently fold in the egg yolks, 25 g (1 oz) crumbled blue cheese and 2 snipped spring onions. Heat 1 teaspoon butter in a medium frying pan, pour in the egg mixture and cook for 1 minute. Sprinkle over 1 tablespoon grated Parmesan cheese and place under a hot grill until golden and just set. Serve with a green salad.

suppers

# vegetable & feta bake

Preparation time **10 minutes**
Cooking time **1 hour**
 **10 minutes**
Serves **4**

4 tablespoons **olive oil**
1 **aubergine**, halved
 and sliced
3 **courgettes**, sliced
1 **onion**, sliced
2 **garlic cloves**, finely sliced
650 g (1 lb 5 oz) **potatoes**,
 scrubbed and cubed
400 g (13 oz) **passata**
250 g (8 oz) **cherry tomatoes**
handful of **fresh herbs**,
 chopped
200 g (7 oz) **feta cheese**,
 crumbled
100 g (3½ oz) **fresh**
 **gluten-free wholemeal**
 **breadcrumbs**
**salt** and **black pepper**

**Heat** the oil in a large frying pan, add the aubergine, courgettes, onion and garlic and fry for 4–5 minutes.

**Add** the potatoes, passata, tomatoes and herbs to the pan and season. Stir well, transfer to a large overnproof dish and place in a preheated oven, 200°C (400°F), Gas Mark 6, for 45 minutes. Remove from the oven.

**Sprinkle** the feta and breadcrumbs over the roasted vegetable mixture, return to the oven and continue to cook for 12–15 minutes until golden.

**For vegetable & prawn bake**, make as above and cook for 45 minutes in the oven. Stir in 300 g (10 oz) raw peeled and deveined tiger prawns, then scatter over 200 g (7 oz) grated Gruyère cheese and the breadcrumbs and continue to cook as above.

# teriyaki beef with rice noodles

Preparation time **15 minutes**, plus marinating
Cooking time **10 minutes**
Serves **4**

500 g (1 lb) **sirloin steak**
300 g (10 oz) **dried rice ribbon noodles**
2 teaspoons **sesame oil**
1 tablespoon peeled and grated **fresh root ginger**
1 **garlic clove**, finely sliced
100 g (3½ oz) **mangetout**, sliced
1 **carrot**, cut into matchsticks
4 **spring onions**, shredded
handful of **coriander**, chopped

**Teriyaki marinade**
2 tablespoons **gluten-free soy sauce**
2 tablespoons **sake**
1 tablespoon **mirin**
½ tablespoon **caster sugar**

**Make** the marinade by mixing together all the ingredients in a small jug. Place the beef in a dish, pour over the marinade, cover and marinate in the refrigerator for at least 2 hours, preferably overnight.

**Soak** the rice noodles in boiling water according to the pack instructions. Drain well.

**Preheat** a griddle, meanwhile, so it is really hot. Place the beef on the griddle, reserving the marinade, and cook for 2–3 minutes on each side. Transfer to a chopping board and leave to rest.

**Heat** the oil in wok or large frying pan, add the ginger and garlic and fry for 30 seconds. Add the vegetables and cook until just beginning to soften.

**Add** the coriander, noodles and 2–3 tablespoons of the marinade and heat through. Spoon on to 4 serving plates, slice the beef and serve on top of the noodles.

**For Thai beef salad**, mix together the marinade ingredients as above, adding 1 teaspoon sesame oil, the grated rind and juice of 1 lime, 3 tablespoons Thai fish sauce, a handful each of chopped coriander, mint and Thai basil. Cover and chill. When ready to serve, griddle the beef as above. Using a peeler, slice ½ cucumber and 2 carrots into ribbons and stir into the chilled dressing with 4 shredded spring onions, 12 halved cherry tomatoes and 200 g (7 oz) salad leaves. Slice the steak thinly, stir into the salad and serve.

# chicken in a pot

Preparation time **10 minutes**
Cooking time **1 hour
30 minutes**
Serves **4**

2 tablespoons **olive oil**
100 g (3½ oz) **streaky
bacon**, chopped
2 **onions**, cut into wedges
500 g (1 lb) **baby carrots**,
halved
600 g (1¼ lb) **new potatoes**,
halved if large
1 **garlic bulb**, halved across
the middle
bunch of **thyme**
1 **fennel bulb**, sliced
1.5 kg (3 lb) **whole chicken**
2 large glasses **dry
white wine**
**salt** and **black pepper**

**Heat** the oil in a large flameproof casserole, add the bacon and fry for 1–2 minutes until beginning to brown. Add all the remaining ingredients and season well.

**Cover** and place in a preheated oven, 200°C (400°F), Gas Mark 6, for 1 hour.

**Remove** the lid and cook for a further 30 minutes or until the juices run clear when the thickest part of the leg is pierced with a knife. Serve with large hunks of crusty gluten-free bread if liked.

**For braised peas**, to serve as an accompaniment, heat 25 g (1 oz) butter and 1 tablespoon olive oil in a large frying pan, add 100 g (3½ oz) chopped bacon or pancetta and fry for 2 minutes or until beginning to crisp. Add 300 g (10 oz) fresh or frozen peas and 100 ml (3½ fl oz) gluten-free chicken stock and cook for 3–4 minutes. Stir in 1 tablespoon chopped mint and the juice of ½ lemon and season well.

# roasted butternut squash risotto

Preparation time **10 minutes**
Cooking time **25 minutes**
Serves **4**

1 **butternut squash**, peeled,
   deseeded and cut into
   2.5 cm (1 inch) cubes
3 tablespoons **olive oil**
handful of **sage leaves**
1 **onion**, chopped
200 g (7 oz) **risotto rice**
1 glass **dry white wine**
600 ml (1 pint) **gluten-free
   vegetable stock**
4 tablespoons grated
   **Parmesan cheese**
15 g (½ oz) **butter**
75 g (3 oz) **blue cheese**,
   crumbled
75 g (3 oz) **rocket leaves**
**salt** and **black pepper**

**Put** the squash on a baking sheet, drizzle over half the oil and scatter over the sage leaves. Place in a preheated oven, 200°C (400°F), Gas Mark 6, for 20–25 minutes until golden and tender.

**Heat** the remaining oil in a large frying pan, while the squash is roasting. Add the onion and fry for 3–4 minutes until softened, then mix in the rice and coat with the oil. Pour in the wine and cook, stirring, until the liquid is absorbed.

**Add** the stock a ladleful at a time, stirring continually, adding the next ladle only once the previous one has been absorbed. When the rice is al dente, remove the pan from the heat, stir in the Parmesan and butter and season well.

**Top** the risotto with the squash and serve in shallow bowls with the blue cheese and rocket scattered over.

**For wild mushroom risotto**, place 15 g (½ oz) dried porcini mushrooms in a jug and pour over boiling water to just cover. Soak for 5 minutes, then chop the mushrooms and sieve the soaking liquid. Omit the squash and cook the risotto as above, adding the mushrooms and liquid with the last addition of stock. Once the rice is al dente, stir in a handful of chopped parsley and serve.

# polenta mini pizzas

Preparation time **10 minutes**
Cooking time **20 minutes**
Makes **10**

600 ml (1 pint) **gluten-free vegetable stock**
150 g (5 oz) **instant polenta**
25 g (1 oz) **Parmesan cheese**, grated

**Topping**
2 large **tomatoes**, sliced
75 g (3 oz) **Parma ham**, roughly torn
150 g (5 oz) **Gorgonzola cheese**, crumbled
50 g (2 oz) **pine nuts**, toasted
1 tablespoon **olive oil**, plus extra for oiling
**handful** of **basil leaves**

**Put** the stock in a saucepan and bring to the boil, then stir in the polenta and Parmesan over a low heat. Continue to cook, stirring, until thick.

**Turn** out on to a lightly oiled surface and spread out to a thickness of 1 cm (½ inch). Using a plain cutter, stamp out 10 rounds a little larger than the tomato slices and place on a lightly oiled baking sheet.

**Top** each 'pizza' with a slice of tomato, some ham, Gorgonzola and pine nuts and drizzle over a little oil.

**Place** in a preheated oven, 220°C (425°F), Gas Mark 7, for 10–12 minutes until golden. Scatter over the basil leaves and serve.

**For tomato, spinach & mozzarella pizzas**, make the polenta pizza bases as above. Replace the large tomatoes with 12 chopped cherry tomatoes and scatter over the pizzas with 100 g (3½ oz) cooked and well-squeezed chopped baby leaf spinach and 150 g (5 oz) torn mozzarella cheese. Drizzle with a little olive oil and scatter over the basil. Cook in the oven, as above.

# chicken tagine

Preparation time **20 minutes**, plus marinating

Cooking time **1 hour 40 minutes**

Serves **4**

8 large skinless **chicken thighs** or 1 **whole chicken**, jointed

1 teaspoon **ground cumin**

1 teaspoon **ground coriander**

½ teaspoon **ground turmeric**

1 teaspoon **ground ginger**

1 teaspoon **paprika**

3 tablespoons **olive oil**

2 **onions**, cut into wedges

2 **garlic cloves**, finely sliced

1 **fennel bulb**, sliced

300 g (10 oz) small **new potatoes**

handful of **sultanas**

8 **ready-to-eat dried apricots**

100 g (3½ oz) **green olives** (optional)

pinch of **saffron threads**

400 ml (14 fl oz) hot **gluten-free chicken stock**

small bunch of **coriander**, chopped

**salt** and **black pepper**

**Slash** each piece of chicken 2–3 times with a small knife. Mix together the spices and half the olive oil, rub over the chicken pieces, cover and marinate in the refrigerator for at least 2 hours, preferably overnight.

**Heat** the remaining oil in a tagine or large flameproof casserole, add the chicken pieces and fry for 4–5 minutes until golden all over. Add the onion, garlic and fennel to the pan and continue to fry for 2–3 minutes.

**Add** all the remaining ingredients, except the coriander, and stir well. Cover and simmer for about 1½ hours or until the chicken begins to fall off the bone. Season well and stir in the coriander.

**For lamb tagine with prunes & almonds**, marinate 600 g (1¼ lb) cubed lean lamb in the spice and olive oil mixture, then continue with the recipe as above but replace the apricots with 8 prunes. Cover and simmer for about 2 hours or until the meat is cooked through and tender. Stir in a handful of toasted flaked almonds with the coriander before serving.

# crusted salmon with tomato salsa

Preparation time **10 minutes**
Cooking time **12–15 minutes**
Serves **4**

1 tablespoon chopped
  **fresh herbs**
1 **garlic clove**, crushed
3 tablespoons **polenta**
4 pieces of **skinless salmon
  fillet**, about 125 g
  (4 oz) each
**black pepper**
4 tablespoons **light crème
  fraîche**, to serve
**green salad**, crushed

**Salsa**
375 g (12 oz) **cherry
  tomatoes**, quartered
1 small **red onion**, finely sliced
½ **red chilli**, deseeded and
  finely chopped
handful of **coriander**, chopped

**Mix** together the herbs, garlic and polenta in a shallow bowl. Coat the salmon pieces in the polenta mix, pressing it down firmly.

**Put** the coated fish on a baking sheet and place in a preheated oven, 200°C (400°F), Gas Mark 6, for 12–15 minutes until cooked through.

**Mix** together the salsa ingredients in a bowl. Place the salmon on 4 serving plates, top with the salsa and a spoonful of crème fraîche, season with black pepper and serve with a green salad.

**For polenta-crusted chicken**, beat together 2 tablespoons cream cheese with the chopped fresh herbs and a peeled, crushed and finely diced clove of garlic. Make a horizontal slit in 4 boneless, skinless chicken breasts. Fill the cavities of the chicken breasts with the cream cheese mixture, then secure with cocktail sticks. Dip the chicken breasts in a little gluten-free flour, a little beaten egg, then in the polenta. Fry in olive oil for 2–3 minutes on each side, transfer to a baking sheet and place in a preheated oven, 200°C (400°F), Gas Mark 6, for 10–12 minutes or until the chicken is cooked through. Serve with the salsa and a green salad.

# lamb kofte with tzatziki & salad

Preparation time **15 minutes**
Cooking time **6–7 minutes**
Serves **4**

500 g (1 lb) **minced lamb**
2 teaspoons **ground cumin**
2 teaspoons **thyme leaves**
1 teaspoon **chilli powder**
grated rind of ½ **lemon**
**salt** and **black pepper**

**Tzatziki**
200 g (7 fl oz) **Greek yogurt**
¼ **cucumber**, grated
handful of **mint**, chopped
juice of ½ **lemon**
1 **garlic clove**, crushed

**Red onion salad**
1 large **red onion**, finely sliced
2 large **tomatoes**, thinly sliced
2 tablespoons **olive oil**
1 tablespoon **red wine vinegar**

**Mix** together the lamb, cumin, thyme, chilli powder and lemon rind in a bowl and season well. Divide the mixture into 8 and shape around 8 metal skewers.

**Place** the skewers under a hot grill or on the barbecue for about 6–7 minutes, turning occasionally, until golden and cooked through.

**Combine** all the tzatziki ingredients in a serving dish. Mix together all the salad ingredients in a serving bowl.

**Serve** the kofte with the tzatziki, red onion salad and toasted gluten-free bread or steamed rice, if liked.

**For spiced chicken skewers**, whisk together the grated rind and juice of 1 orange, 1 teaspoon peeled and grated fresh root ginger, 1 tablespoon gluten-free soy sauce, 1 tablespoon sesame oil, 1 tablespoon runny honey and 1 teaspoon dried chilli flakes in a bowl. Stir in 3 cubed boneless, skinless chicken breasts and marinate in the refrigerator for at least 20 minutes. Thread the chicken on to skewers with red onion wedges and chunks of red pepper. Place under a hot grill or on the barbecue for 5–6 minutes, or until beginning to char and cooked through.

# chicken & leek gratin

Preparation time **15 minutes**
Cooking time **40–45 minutes**
Serves **4**

1 tablespoon **olive oil**
1 **onion**, chopped
1 **garlic clove**, crushed
4 **leeks**, trimmed, cleaned
  and chopped
4 **boneless, skinless chicken
  breasts**, cut into chunks
1 small glass **dry white wine**
1 tablespoon **rice flour**
300 ml (½ pint) **gluten-free
  chicken stock**
150 ml (¼ pint) **double cream**
2 tablespoons chopped
  **tarragon**
1 tablespoon **gluten-free
  English mustard**
200 g (7 oz) **fresh gluten-free
  breadcrumbs**
100 g (3½ oz) **Gruyère
  cheese**, grated
**salt** and **black pepper**

**Heat** the oil in a large saucepan, add the onion, garlic and leeks and fry for 3–4 minutes. Transfer the vegetables to a plate, add the chicken to the pan and fry for 3 minutes until beginning to colour all over.

**Add** the wine and simmer until it has reduced by about half. Add the flour and cook, stirring, for 1 minute, then gradually add the stock and cook, stirring all the time, until the sauce has thickened.

**Stir** in the leek mixture, cream, tarragon and mustard and season well. Transfer to an ovenproof dish, then sprinkle over the breadcrumbs and Gruyère.

**Place** in a preheated oven, 200°C (400°F), Gas Mark 6, for 25–30 minutes until golden and bubbling. Serve with steamed vegetables.

**For chicken & mushroom pasta bake**, cook 375 g (12 oz) gluten-free pasta shapes in a saucepan of salted boiling water according to the pack instructions, then drain well. Meanwhile, fry the onion and garlic as above, with 500 g (1 lb) mixed sliced mushrooms. Continue as above, stirring the mushroom mixture into the sauce with the cream, tarragon and mustard. Season well and add the pasta, then transfer to an ovenproof dish, sprinkle over the breadcrumbs and Gruyère and bake as above.

# seafood noodles

Preparation time **10 minutes**
Cooking time **7–10 minutes**
Serves **4**

375 g (12 oz) **dried rice ribbon noodles**
3 tablespoons **olive oil**
1 small **onion**, finely chopped
3 **garlic cloves**, crushed
5 cm (2 inch) **fresh root ginger**, peeled and finely grated
1 **red chilli**, deseeded and finely chopped
200 g (7 oz) **cherry tomatoes**, quartered
500 g (1 lb) **raw tiger prawns**, peeled and deveined
200 g (7 oz) **fresh white crab meat**
3 tablespoons chopped **parsley**

**Soak** the noodles in boiling water according to the pack instructions. Drain well.

**Meanwhile** heat the oil in a large frying pan, add the onion, garlic, ginger and chilli and fry for 1–2 minutes until softened.

**Add** the tomatoes and prawns and cook for 2–3 minutes or until the prawns are cooked through and piping hot.

**Stir** in the crab meat and parsley, combine with the noodles and serve immediately.

**For hearty seafood laksa,** cook the onion, garlic, chilli and ginger as above. Process ½ teaspoon turmeric and the inner stems of 2 lemon grass stalks in a small food processor or blender to a paste. Gently fry the lemon grass paste with the onion mixture, for 2 minutes, then add 400 ml (14 fl oz) can coconut milk and 1 litre (1¾ pints) gluten-free fish or vegetable stock and simmer for 10 minutes. Stir in 500 g (1 lb) cooked peeled and deveined tiger prawns, 200 g (7 oz) fresh white crab meat, 2 tablespoons chopped coriander and 250 g (8 oz) soaked rice noodles. Heat through and serve.

# fruity stuffed peppers

Preparation time **15 minutes**
Cooking time **1 hour**
Serves **4**

2 **red peppers**, cored,
  deseeded and halved
2 **orange peppers**, cored,
  deseeded and halved
2 tablespoons **olive oil**, plus
  extra for brushing
1 **red onion**, chopped
1 **garlic clove**, crushed
1 small **red chilli**, deseeded
  and finely chopped
25 g (1 oz) **pine nuts**
200 g (7 oz) cooked **wild rice**
400 g (13 oz) can **green
  lentils**, drained and rinsed
250 g (8 oz) **cherry tomatoes**,
  quartered
100 g (3½ oz) **ready-to-eat
  dried apricots**, chopped
handful of **sultanas**
grated rind of 1 **lemon**
2 tablespoons chopped
  **fresh herbs**
100 g (3 ½ oz) **feta cheese**,
  crumbled

**Put** the peppers in an ovenproof dish, cut side up, and brush each with a little oil. Place in a preheated oven, 200°C (400°F), Gas Mark 6, for 20 minutes.

**Heat** the oil in frying pan, add the onion, garlic and chilli and fry for 2 minutes, then add the pine nuts and cook for a further 2 minutes until golden. Stir in all the remaining ingredients.

**Remove** the peppers from the oven and spoon the stuffing mixture into the peppers. Cover with foil, return to the oven and cook for 25 minutes, then remove the foil and cook for a further 15 minutes. Serve with a crisp salad.

**For fruity stuffed aubergines**, roughly prick 2 large aubergines all over with a fork. Place on a baking sheet and put in a preheated oven, 200°C, (400°F), Gas Mark 6, for 30 minutes. Remove from the oven and halve lengthways, scoop out most of the flesh and roughly chop. Make the stuffing as above, adding the aubergine flesh to the pan with the onion, garlic and chilli. Spoon the mixture into the aubergine skins and cook as above.

# bacon & spinach pasta

Preparation time **10 minutes**
Cooking time **15 minutes**
Serves **4**

375 g (12 oz) **gluten-free pasta**
1 tablespoon **olive oil**
200 g (7 oz) **streaky bacon**, sliced
1 **onion**, sliced
2 tablespoons **pine nuts**
175 g (6 oz) **baby leaf spinach**
300 g (10 oz) **cherry tomatoes**, halved
6 tablespoons **single cream**
2 tablespoons grated **Parmesan cheese**
4 **spring onions**, sliced
**salt** and **black pepper**

**Cook** the pasta in a saucepan of salted boiling water according to the pack instructions. Drain well.

**Heat** the oil in a frying pan, add the bacon and onion and fry for 3–4 minutes until the bacon is crisp and the onion softened.

**Add** the pine nuts and cook for 1 minute. Stir in the spinach and tomatoes and cook until the spinach is just wilted.

**Stir** the spinach mixture into the pasta. Mix in the cream, Parmesan and spring onions, season well and serve immediately.

**For broccoli, bacon & blue cheese pasta**, cook the pasta as above, adding 300 g (10 oz) broccoli florets 4 minutes before the end of cooking time. Drain well. Meanwhile, fry the bacon as above, omitting the onion. Stir in 150 ml (¼ pint) single cream and 100 g (3 ½ oz) crumbled blue cheese. Mix into the pasta and broccoli and serve immediately.

# thai coconut chicken

Preparation time **20 minutes**
Cooking time **40–45 minutes**
Serves **4**

500 ml (17 fl oz) **gluten-free chicken stock**
4 **boneless, skinless chicken breasts,** cubed
1 tablespoon **groundnut oil**
400 ml (14 fl oz) can **coconut milk**
**salt** and **black pepper**
roughly chopped **coriander,** to garnish
**cooked rice ribbon noodles,** or **fragrant rice,** to serve

**Curry paste**
1 **green chilli,** deseeded and roughly chopped
1 small **onion,** roughly chopped
3 **garlic cloves,** chopped
50 g (2 oz) **coriander**
2 teaspoons **Thai fish sauce**
¼ teaspoon **ground turmeric**
1 **lemon grass stalk,** roughly chopped
grated rind and juice of 1 **lime**
2 teaspoons **caster sugar**
15 g (½ oz) **fresh root ginger,** peeled and roughly chopped

**Make** the curry paste. Put all the paste ingredients in a food processor or blender and blitz until smooth, scraping the mixture down from the side of the bowl if necessary.

**Put** the stock and curry paste in a large saucepan and bring to the boil. Cook, uncovered, for 15–20 minutes until most of the liquid has evaporated.

**Season** the chicken lightly. Heat the oil in a large frying pan, add the chicken and gently fry for 5 minutes.

**Add** the chicken and coconut milk to the reduced curry sauce and cook for about 20 minutes until the chicken is very tender. Ladle into shallow bowls, sprinkle with coriander and serve with fragrant rice or rice noodles.

**For Thai coconut tofu**, make the curry paste as above, replacing the fish sauce with 2 teaspoons gluten-free soy sauce. Continue as above, replacing the chicken stock with 500 ml (17 fl oz) gluten-free vegetable stock and the chicken with 200 g (7 oz) cubed firm tofu.

# harissa salmon with sweet potato

Preparation time **10 minutes**, plus marinating
Cooking time **35–40 minutes**
Serves **4**

2 tablespoons **natural yogurt**
2 teaspoons **harissa**
2 tablespoons chopped **coriander**, plus extra to garnish
grated rind and juice of ½ **lime**
4 pieces of **skinless salmon fillet**, about 150 g (5 oz) each
**vegetable oil**, for oiling
**lime wedges** and **flat-leaf parsley**, to serve

**Spicy sweet potato**
500 g (1 lb) **sweet potato**, peeled and cut into chunks
1 tablespoon **olive oil**
1 teaspoon **cumin seeds**
½ teaspoon **garam masala**
**salt** and **black pepper**

**Mix** together the yogurt, harissa, coriander and lime rind and juice in a non-metallic bowl. Add the salmon and coat in the mixture. Cover and marinate in the refrigerator for at least 20 minutes.

**Toss** together the sweet potato chunks, olive oil, cumin seeds and garam masala in a bowl and season well. Put in a roasting tin and place in a preheated oven, 200°C (400°F), Gas Mark 6, for 35–40 minutes until golden.

**Heat** a lightly oiled frying pan or griddle until hot towards the end of the sweet potato roasting time. Add the salmon and cook for 3 minutes on each side until just cooked. Garnish with coriander and serve with the sweet potatoes, lime wedges and flat-leaf parsley.

**For spiced chicken drumsticks**, make the yogurt and harissa marinade as above and stir in 1 teaspoon groundnut oil. Pierce the flesh of 8 skinless chicken drumsticks several times, then cover with the marinade. Marinate as above, then place under a hot grill or on a barbecue for 12–15 minutes until cooked through and beginning to char. Serve with a salad.

# loin of pork with lentils

Preparation time **15 minutes**
Cooking time about **1 hour 55 minutes**, plus resting
Serves **5–6**

175 g (6 oz) **Puy lentils**
875 g (1¾ lb) **pork loin**, rind removed, boned and rolled
2 tablespoons **olive oil**
2 large **onions**, sliced
3 **garlic cloves**, sliced
1 tablespoon finely chopped **rosemary**
300 ml (½ pint) **gluten-free chicken** or **vegetable stock**
250 g (8 oz) **baby carrots**, scrubbed and left whole
**salt** and **black pepper**

**Put** the lentils in a saucepan, cover with water and bring to the boil. Boil rapidly for 10 minutes, then drain well.

**Sprinkle** the pork with salt and pepper. Heat the oil in a large heavy-based frying pan and brown the meat on all sides. Transfer to a casserole dish and add the lentils.

**Add** the onions to the pan and fry for 5 minutes. Stir in the garlic, rosemary and stock and bring to the boil. Pour over the meat and lentils and cover with a lid. Place in a preheated oven, 180°C (350°F), Gas Mark 4, for 1 hour.

**Stir** the carrots into the casserole, season well and return to the oven for a further 20–30 minutes until the pork is cooked through and the lentils are soft. Drain the meat, transfer to a serving platter and leave to rest in a warm place for 20 minutes. Carve into thin slices, then serve with the lentils, carrots and juices.

**For apricot stuffed pork**, heat 1 tablespoon olive oil in a frying pan, add 1 chopped onion and 1 crushed garlic clove and fry for 3–4 minutes until softened. Stir in 100 g (3½ oz) finely chopped ready-to-eat dried apricots, 2 tablespoons pine nuts, 1 tablespoon chopped sage and 2 tablespoons fresh gluten-free breadcrumbs. Remove from the heat, stir to combine, then spread inside the pork before rolling up and tying at intervals along its length with kitchen string. Follow the recipe above, but cook the stuffed pork with the lentils in the oven for about 1¼ before adding the carrots and cooking for a further 20–30 minutes as above.

# wild rice & griddled chicken salad

Preparation time **10 minutes**, plus marinating
Cooking time **35 minutes**
Serves **4**

1 **garlic clove**, crushed
2 teaspoons **olive oil**
1 teaspoon **balsamic vinegar**
4 small **boneless, skinless chicken breasts**, halved horizontally

**Rice salad**
200 g (7 oz) mixed **wild** and **basmati rice**
2 **red peppers**, roasted, cored, deseeded and sliced
3 **spring onions**, sliced
125 g (4 oz) **cherry tomatoes**, quartered
75 g (3 oz) **rocket leaves**
75g (3 oz) **soft goats' cheese**, crumbled

**Dressing**
juice of ½ **lemon**
1 teaspoon **gluten-free Dijon mustard**
1 teaspoon **runny honey**
2 tablespoons **olive oil**

**Mix** together the garlic, olive oil and vinegar in a non-metallic bowl, add the chicken and coat in the marinade. Cover and leave to marinate in the refrigerator for at least 30 minutes.

**Cook** the rice in a saucepan of boiling water according to the pack instructions. Drain well and leave to cool, then mix with the peppers, spring onions, tomatoes, rocket and goats' cheese in a large bowl.

**Whisk** together the dressing ingredients in a bowl and stir into the rice salad. Spoon the salad on to 4 serving plates.

**Heat** a griddle pan until hot and cook the chicken for 3–4 minutes on each side until cooked through. Immediately before serving, slice the griddled chicken and arrange on top of the salad.

**For wild rice, orange & haloumi salad**, make the rice salad as above, replacing the red peppers with the sliced flesh of 2 oranges and omitting the goats' cheese. Make the dressing as above and stir into the salad. Cut 200 g (7 oz) haloumi cheese into slices, brush with a little olive oil and season with plenty of black pepper. Heat a griddle pan until hot and cook the haloumi for 1–2 minutes on each side until browned. Arrange on top of the rice salad and serve.

# spinach & fish pie

Preparation time **15 minutes**
Cooking time **45–55 minutes**
Serves **4**

1 tablespoon **olive oil**
1 **onion**, chopped
175 g (6 oz) **baby leaf
  spinach**
50 g (2 oz) **butter**
25 g (1 oz) **rice flour**
600 ml (1 pint) **milk**
1 tablespoon **gluten-free
  wholegrain mustard**
good grating of **nutmeg**
650 g (1 lb 5 oz) mixed
  **skinless salmon, haddock**
  and **smoked haddock
  fillets**, cut into chunks
200 g (7 oz) **raw prawns**,
  peeled and deveined
**salt** and **black pepper**

**Potato topping**
1 kg (2 lb) **potatoes**, peeled
  and cut into chunks
good knob of **butter**
100 ml (3½ fl oz) **single
  cream**

**Make** the potato topping. Cook the potatoes in a saucepan of salted boiling water for 15 minutes or until tender. Drain well and return to the pan. Mash together with the butter and cream and season well.

**Heat** the oil in a large saucepan, add the onion and fry for 2–3 minutes until beginning to soften. Add the spinach to the pan and cook until wilted and any liquid has evaporated.

**Melt** the butter in a saucepan, add the flour and cook, stirring, for 1 minute. Gradually add the milk and cook, stirring all the time, until thickened and smooth. Stir in the mustard and nutmeg and season well.

**Arrange** the fish and the prawns in a large ovenproof dish. Pour the sauce over the fish, spoon the mash on top and place in a preheated oven, 200°C (400°F), Gas Mark 6, for 30–35 minutes until golden and bubbling.

**For rosti-topped fish pie**, steam 3 peeled baking potatoes for 12–15 minutes, then grate into a large bowl. Stir in 25 g (1 oz) melted butter and season well. Make the sauce as above and pour over the fish and prawns in a large ovenproof dish. Scatter the rosti over the fish and sauce and cook as above.

# chilli rice noodles

Preparation time **10 minutes**
Cooking time **7–10 minutes**
Serves **4**

8 teaspoons **seasoned rice vinegar**
2 tablespoons **caster sugar**
2 teaspoons **Thai fish sauce**
2 tablespoons **gluten-free soy sauce**
200 g (7 oz) **dried rice ribbon noodles**
2 tablespoons **vegetable** or **groundnut oil**
1 **red chilli**, deseeded and finely shredded
1 large **red pepper**, cored, deseeded and finely shredded
100 g (3½ oz) **mangetout**, thinly sliced lengthways

**Mix** together the vinegar, sugar, fish sauce and soy sauce in a bowl.

**Soak** the noodles in boiling water according to the pack instructions.

**Heat** the oil in a frying pan while the noodles are soaking, add the chilli, red pepper and mangetout and fry for 4–5 minutes until softened.

**Drain** the noodles and add to the pan with the vinegar mixture. Toss together and serve immediately.

**For chilli chicken & baby corn noodles**, mix together the vinegar, sugar, fish sauce and soy sauce and soak the noodles as above. Heat the oil in a frying pan, add 3 sliced boneless, skinless chicken breasts and fry for 2–3 minutes until beginning to brown. Add the chilli, red pepper, mangetout and 100 g (3½ oz) baby sweetcorn and fry for a further 3 minutes. Combine with the drained noodles and vinegar mixture as above.

# spring lamb stew & dumplings

Preparation time **15 minutes**
Cooking time **1 hour 45 minutes**
Serves **4**

2 tablespoons **gluten-free plain flour**
750 g (1 ½ lb) **lean lamb**, cubed
2 tablespoons **olive oil**
12 **shallots**, peeled
2 **garlic cloves**, sliced
1 tablespoon **tomato purée**
**thyme** sprig
1 **bay leaf**
300 ml (½ pint) **red wine**
600 ml (1 pint) **gluten-free chicken stock**
750 g (1 ½ lb) cooked **baby carrots**, peeled and chopped **turnips** and **new potatoes**
200 g (7 oz) **French beans**, topped and tailed
**salt** and **black pepper**

**Dumplings**
175 g (6 oz) **rice flour**
1 teaspoon **gluten-free baking powder**
75 g (3 oz) **gluten-free suet**
handful of **fresh herbs**, chopped

**Season** the flour well, then toss the lamb in the flour. Heat the oil in a large flameproof casserole, add the meat in batches and fry until browned all over.

**Add** the shallots and garlic and fry for 1 minute, then stir in the tomato purée, thyme and bay leaf.

**Stir** in the red wine and stock gradually, bring to a gentle simmer, then cover and cook for 1 hour or until the meat is almost tender.

**Make** the dumplings. Mix together all the ingredients in a large bowl, season and then add enough cold water to make a soft dough. Shape into 12 balls.

**Stir** the vegetables into the stew, then top with the dumplings. Cover and continue to cook for 25–30 minutes until the vegetables are tender.

**For sweet potato & aubergine stew**, omit the lamb and fry the shallots and garlic with 2 large peeled and cubed sweet potatoes and 1 chopped aubergine for 4–5 minutes until beginning to soften. Continue as above, replacing the chicken stock with a 600 ml (1 pint) gluten-free vegetable stock. Gently simmer for 20 minutes, then add 150 g (5 oz) French beans just before topping with the dumplings. Cover and cook for a further 25–30 minutes.

# spiced haddock & cumin potatoes

Preparation time **10 minutes**, plus marinating

Cooking time **40 minutes**

Serves **4**

4 pieces of **haddock fillet**, about 150 g (5 oz) each

**Spice rub**

½ teaspoon **paprika**

1 teaspoon **ground cumin**

1 **garlic clove**, crushed

5 cm (2 inch) **fresh root ginger**, peeled and finely grated

½ teaspoon **ground coriander**

1 tablespoon chopped **coriander**

½ teaspoon **turmeric**

1 tablespoon **olive oil**

**Cumin potatoes**

500 g (1 lb) **potatoes**, peeled and cut into chunks

1 teaspoon **cumin seeds**

1 **garlic bulb**, broken up into cloves

1 tablespoon **olive oil**

**salt** and **black pepper**

**Place** the fish in a dish. Mix together all the spice rub ingredients in a bowl and rub into the fish. Cover and marinate in the refrigerator for 30 minutes.

**Mix** all the cumin potato ingredients together and put on a baking sheet. Place in a preheated oven, 200°C (400°F), Gas Mark 6, for about 40 minutes or until crisp and golden.

**Heat** a griddle or frying pan until hot and cook the fish for 2 minutes on each side until crisp and golden. Serve with the potatoes and a mixed salad.

**For homemade coleslaw**, to serve as an accompaniment, grate 3 peeled carrots into a large bowl. Finely shred 1 small white or red cabbage and stir into the carrots with 1 small sliced onion. Whisk together 4 tablespoons light crème fraîche, 1 tablespoon chopped coriander, 1 teaspoon cumin seeds and the grated rind and juice of ½ lemon in a bowl and stir into the coleslaw.

# pancetta risotto with chicken

Preparation time **10 minutes**
Cooking time **25 minutes**
Serves **4**

1 tablespoon **olive oil**, plus
extra for drizzling
150 g (5 oz) **pancetta**, sliced
or cubed
1 small **onion**, finely chopped
1 **garlic clove**, chopped
300 g (10 oz) **risotto rice**
125 ml (4 fl oz) **dry white
wine**
900 ml (1½ pints) **gluten-free
chicken stock**
125 g (4 oz) **petit pois**
1 teaspoon **thyme leaves**
4 small **boneless**, **skinless
chicken breasts**, halved
horizontally
2 tablespoons grated
**Parmesan cheese**
**salt** and **black pepper**

**Heat** the oil in a large frying pan, add the pancetta and fry for 2 minutes until beginning to brown. Stir in the onion and garlic and continue to fry for 1−2 minutes until softened.

**Mix** in the rice and coat with the oil. Pour in the wine and stir until the liquid is absorbed.

**Add** the stock a ladleful at a time, stirring continually, adding the next ladle only once the previous one has been absorbed. With the last addition of stock, stir in the peas and thyme.

**Heat** a griddle until hot when almost ready to serve. Drizzle a little olive oil over the chicken and cook for 2−3 minutes on each side until cooked through. Slice the chicken into the risotto.

**Stir** the Parmesan into the risotto when the rice is al dente and the peas are tender. Ladle into shallow bowls and top with the chicken. Season well.

**For risotto cakes**, make the risotto as above, then leave to cool completely. Once cooled, stir in 1 small egg or 1 large egg yolk and form the mixture into 8 'cakes'. Roll each risotto cake in fresh gluten-free breadcrumbs, then fry in oil for 2 minutes on each side or until golden and heated through. Serve with salad.

# aubergine bake

Preparation time **10 minutes**
Cooking time **40–45 minutes**
Serves **4**

2 large **aubergines**, sliced
2 tablespoons **olive oil**
150 g (5 oz) **mozzarella
    cheese**, roughly chopped
4 tablespoons grated
    **Parmesan cheese**
**salt** and **black pepper**

**Tomato sauce**
1 tablespoon **olive oil**
1 **garlic clove**, crushed
1 small **onion**, finely chopped
400 g (13 oz) can **plum
    tomatoes**
handful of **basil**, torn

**Make** the tomato sauce. Heat the oil in a saucepan, add the garlic and onion and fry for 3–4 minutes until softened. Add the tomatoes and basil, bring to the boil and simmer for 15 minutes.

**Brush** the aubergines with the oil on each side while the sauce is simmering. Heat a griddle until hot and cook the aubergine slices for 1–2 minutes on each side until tender and browned.

**Spoon** a little of the tomato sauce into an ovenproof dish, layer over half the aubergines, scatter over half the mozzarella and Parmesan and season well. Repeat the layering with the remaining ingredients, finishing with a scattering of the cheeses.

**Place** in a preheated oven, 200°C (400°F), Gas Mark 6, for 20–25 minutes until golden and bubbling. Serve with salad and crusty bread.

**For aubergine, chilli & chicken bake**, make the tomato sauce as above, adding 1 deseeded and finely sliced red chilli with the garlic and onion. Cook the aubergine and layer the bake as above, interspersing 300 g (10 oz) torn cooked chicken between the aubergine layers. Cook in the oven as above.

# fish cakes & fennel mayonnaise

Preparation time **20 minutes**
Cooking time **25–30 minutes**
Serves **4**

500 g (1 lb) **skinless cod** or
  **haddock fillets**
4 tablespoons **milk**
750 g (1½ lb) **baking
  potatoes**, peeled and cut
  into chunks
25 g (1 oz) **butter**
2 tablespoons **capers**, rinsed
  and chopped
1 **egg**, beaten
75 g (3 oz) **polenta**
**sunflower** or **olive oil**,
  for frying
**salt** and **black pepper**
**large bunch of watercress**
  to serve

**Fennel mayonnaise**
6 tablespoons **mayonnaise**
3 tablespoons **natural yogurt**
3 tablespoons chopped **fennel**
2 teaspoons **hot horseradish
  sauce**

**Cut** the fish into chunky pieces and put in a frying pan with the milk and a little seasoning. Cover and cook gently for 5 minutes until just cooked through. Drain, reserving the cooking juices.

**Cook** the potatoes in a saucepan of salted boiling water for 15 minutes or until tender. Drain well, tip into a bowl and mash with a fork into chunky pieces.

**Add** the butter, capers, fish and 2 tablespoons of the reserved cooking juices and season well. Mix together until the ingredients are combined but the fish and potatoes are still chunky. Shape the mixture into 8–10 balls and flatten into cakes.

**Put** the egg on a plate and sprinkle the polenta on to another plate. Coat the fish cakes first in the egg and then in the polenta.

**Mix** together the fennel mayonnaise ingredients in a serving dish. Heat 5 mm (½ inch) of oil in a large frying pan and fry the fish cakes, in batches if necessary, for about 2 minutes on each side until golden.

**Serve** the mayonnaise with the hot fish cakes and a little watercress on the side.

**For salmon fishcake & coriander mayonnaise**, make as above, replacing the white fish with 500 g (1 lb) skinless salmon fillets and adding the grated zest of 1 lime to the mixture. Mix the mayonnaise and yogurt with 3 tablespoons of finely chopped coriander and a squeeze of lime juice. Fry the fish cakes as above and serve with the coriander mayonnaise.

# potato pizza margherita

Preparation time **20 minutes**, plus cooling
Cooking time **45 minutes**
Serves **3–4**

1 kg (2 lb) **baking potatoes**, peeled and cut into small chunks
3 tablespoons **olive oil**, plus extra for oiling
1 **egg**, beaten
50 g (2 oz) **Parmesan** or **Cheddar cheese**, grated
4 tablespoons **sun-dried tomato paste** or **tomato ketchup**
500 g (1 lb) **small tomatoes**, thinly sliced
125 g (4 oz) **mozzarella cheese**, thinly sliced
1 tablespoon chopped **thyme**, plus extra sprigs to garnish (optional)
**salt**

**Cook** the potatoes in a saucepan of salted boiling water for 15 minutes or until tender. Drain well, return to the pan and leave to cool for 10 minutes.

**Add** 2 tablespoons of the oil, the egg and half the grated Parmesan to the potato and mix well. Turn out on to an oiled baking sheet and spread out to form a 25 cm (10 inch) round. Place in a preheated oven, 200°C (400°F), Gas Mark 6, for 15 minutes.

**Remove** from the oven and spread with the tomato paste or ketchup. Arrange the tomato and mozzarella slices on top. Scatter with the remaining grated Parmesan, thyme, if using, and a little salt. Drizzle with the remaining oil.

**Return** to the oven for a further 15 minutes until the potato is crisp around the edges and the cheese is melting. Cut into generous wedges, garnish with thyme sprigs, if liked, and serve.

**For corn & salami pizza**, make as above, adding a 200 g (7 oz) can drained sweetcorn and 6 slices of chopped salami with the tomato and mozzarella to the top of the pizza. Continue as above.

# vegetable spaghetti bolognese

1 tablespoon **vegetable oil**
1 **onion**, finely chopped
1 **garlic clove**, finely chopped
1 **celery stick**, finely chopped
1 **carrot**, finely chopped
75 g (3 oz) **chestnut mushrooms**, roughly chopped
1 tablespoon **tomato purée**
400 g (13 oz) can **chopped tomatoes**
250 ml (8 fl oz) **red wine** or **gluten-free vegetable stock**
pinch of **dried mixed herbs**
1 teaspoon **yeast extract**
150 g (5 oz) **textured vegetable protein (TVP)**
2 tablespoons chopped **parsley**
200 g (7 oz) **gluten-free spaghetti**
**salt** and **black pepper**
grated **Parmesan cheese**, to serve

**Heat** the oil in a large heavy-based saucepan over a medium heat. Add the onion, garlic, celery, carrot and mushrooms and cook, stirring frequently, for 5 minutes or until softened. Add the tomato purée and cook, stirring, for a further minute.

**Add** the tomatoes, wine or stock, herbs, yeast extract and TVP. Bring to the boil, then reduce the heat, cover and simmer for 30–40 minutes until the TVP is tender. Stir in the parsley and season well.

**Cook** the pasta in a large saucepan of salted boiling water according to the pack instructions until it is al dente. Drain well.

**Divide** the pasta between 2 serving plates, top with the vegetable mixture and serve immediately with a scattering of grated Parmesan.

**For lentil bolognese**, make the sauce as above, replacing the mushrooms with 1 cored, deseeded and diced red pepper and 150 g (5 oz) canned green lentils. Rinse the lentils well before use. If you are using dried lentils, cook them in boiling water first, according to the package instructions, then drain. Cook the spaghetti as above and serve with the sauce, sprinkled with grated Parmesan cheese.

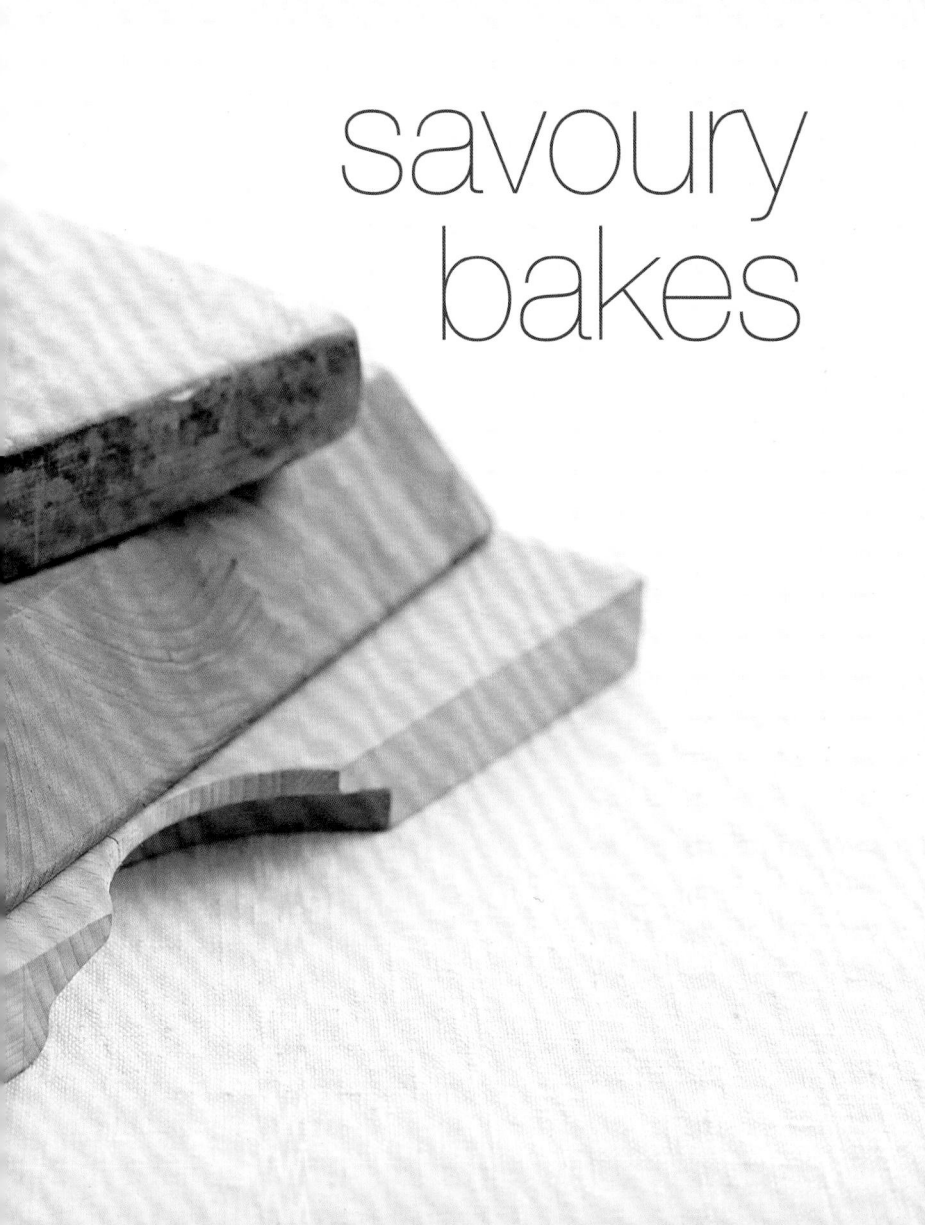

# savoury bakes

# cheesy herby muffins

Preparation time  **5 minutes**
Cooking time  **20 minutes**
Makes **8**

175 g (6 oz) **Gruyère cheese**
3 **spring onions**, finely sliced
1 teaspoon **thyme leaves**
1 tablespoon chopped **parsley**
100 g (3½ oz) **rice flour**
½ teaspoon **gluten-free baking powder**
150 g (5 oz) **fresh gluten-free breadcrumbs**
1 teaspoon **gluten-free English mustard**
3 **eggs**, beaten
50 g (2 oz) **butter**, melted
4 tablespoons **milk**

**Line** a muffin tray with 8 muffin cases.

**Mix** together all the ingredients in a large bowl until just combined and spoon the mixture into the muffin cases.

**Place** in a preheated oven, 190°C (170°F), Gas Mark 5, for 20 minutes or until golden and just firm to the touch. Remove from the oven and serve warm.

### For caramelized onion & feta muffins, heat
1 tablespoon olive oil in a saucepan, add 1 thinly sliced onion and fry over a low heat for about 10 minutes until very soft and beginning to brown. Add 1 teaspoon caster sugar and continue to cook for 2–3 minutes. Line a muffin tray as above. Mix together 100 g (3½ oz) crumbled feta cheese, 1 tablespoon chopped thyme and the caramelized onion with the rice flour, baking powder, breadcrumbs, mustard, eggs, melted butter and milk as above. Spoon into the muffin cases and place in a preheated oven, 200°C (400°F), Gas Mark 6, for 20 minutes until golden and firm to the touch. Serve warm.

# chilli corn bread

Preparation time **5 minutes**
Cooking time **30–35 minutes**
Makes **16 squares**

150 g (5 oz) **rice flour**
150 g (5 oz) **polenta**
1 teaspoon **salt**
2 teaspoons **gluten-free baking powder**
1 tablespoon **caster sugar**
3 tablespoons grated **Parmesan cheese**
handful of **fresh herbs**, chopped
1 **red chilli**, deseeded and finely chopped
3 tablespoons **olive oil,** plus extra for oiling
2 **eggs**, beaten
300 ml (½ pint) **buttermilk**

**Oil** a 20 cm (8 inch) square cake tin.

**Sift** together the flour, polenta, salt and baking powder into a large bowl. Stir in the sugar, Parmesan, herbs and chilli.

**Mix** together the oil, eggs and buttermilk in a separate bowl, then gently stir into the dry ingredients until combined.

**Pour** the mixture into the prepared tin and place in a preheated oven, 190°C (375°F), Gas Mark 5, for 30–35 minutes until golden. Remove from the oven and transfer to a wire rack to cool, then cut into 16 squares. Delicious served with the Fish Chowder on page 48. The bread is best eaten on the same day.

**For bacon & sweetcorn bread**, stir a 200 g (7 oz) can drained sweetcorn and 6 grilled chopped bacon rashers into the dry ingredients and continue as above.

# feta & herb loaf

Preparation time **10 minutes**, plus proving
Cooking time **45 minutes**
Makes **1 x 900 g (2 lb) loaf**

**vegetable oil**, for oiling
200 g (7 oz) **polenta**
100 g (3½ oz) **rice flour**
50 g (2 oz) **dried milk powder**
pinch of **salt**
7 g (¼ oz) sachet **fast-action dried yeast**
2 teaspoons **caster sugar**
2 teaspoons **xanthan gum**
3 **eggs**, beaten
2 tablespoons chopped **fresh herbs**
450 ml (¾ pint) **hand-hot water**
100 g (3½ oz) **feta cheese**, crumbled

**Oil** and line a 900 g (2 lb) loaf tin.

**Sift** together the polenta, flour, milk powder and salt in a large bowl and stir well to combine. Stir in the yeast, sugar and xanthan gum.

**Mix** together the eggs, herbs and water in a separate bowl, add to the dry ingredients and combine to form a smooth mixture. Beat for 5 minutes, then stir in the feta.

**Spoon** the mixture into the prepared tin, cover with a clean damp tea towel and leave in a warm place to rise for about 30 minutes until the mixture is near the top of the tin.

**Place** in a preheated oven, 180°C (350°F), Gas Mark 4, for about 45 minutes or until the loaf is brown and sounds hollow when tapped on the bottom. Remove from the oven and transfer to a wire rack to cool.

**For pesto & parmesan bread**, make as above, replacing the feta with 2 tablespoons grated Parmesan cheese. Stir 2 tablespoons pesto into the egg and water mixture before adding to the dry ingredients. Continue as above.

# nutty seed loaf

Preparation time **10 minutes**
Cooking time **25 minutes**
Makes **8 pieces**

400 g (13 oz) **brown rice flour**, plus extra for dusting
25 g (1 oz) **rice bran**
2 tablespoons **skimmed dried milk powder**
½ teaspoon **bicarbonate of soda**
1 teaspoon **gluten-free baking powder**
½–1 teaspoon **salt**
1 teaspoon **xanthan gum**
pinch of **caster sugar**
50 g (2 oz) mixed **sunflower** and **pumpkin seeds**
50 g (2 oz) **hazelnuts**, toasted and roughly chopped
1 **egg**, lightly beaten
300 ml (½ pint) **buttermilk**

**Stir** together all the dry ingredients, including the nuts, in a large bowl. Mix together the egg and buttermilk in a separate bowl, add to the dry ingredients and combine to form a soft dough.

**Turn** the dough out on to a surface lightly dusted with rice flour and form into a round about 20 cm (8 inches) in diameter. Mark into 8 segments, then place on a baking sheet and dust with a little extra rice flour.

**Place** in an oven preheated to its highest setting and bake for 10 minutes, then reduce the heat to 200°C (400°F), Gas Mark 6, and continue to cook for about 15 minutes until the loaf is golden and sounds hollow when tapped on the bottom. Remove from the oven and transfer to a wire rack to cool.

**For fruity seed loaf,** make the dough as above, adding 100 g (3½ oz) chopped dried figs and 6 chopped ready-to-eat dried apricots to the dry ingredients. Form into a round and bake as above, then brush the top of the loaf with 1 tablespoon runny honey.

# parmesan, olive & tomato loaf

Preparation time **10 minutes**,
plus proving

Cooking time **45 minutes**

Makes **1 x 900 g (2 lb) loaf**

**vegetable oil**, for oiling

200 g (7 oz) **polenta**

100 g (3½ oz) **rice flour**

50 g (2 oz) **dried milk powder**

pinch of **salt**

7 g (¼ oz) sachet **fast-action dried yeast**

2 teaspoons **caster sugar**

2 teaspoons **xanthan gum**

3 **eggs**, beaten

2 tablespoons **sun-dried tomato paste**

450 ml (¾ pint) **hand-hot water**

50 g (2 oz) **Parmesan cheese**, grated

50 g (2 oz) pitted **olives**, chopped

2 teaspoons chopped **oregano**

**Oil** and line a 900 g (2 lb) loaf tin.

**Sift** together the polenta, flour, milk powder and salt into a large bowl and stir well to combine. Stir in the yeast, sugar and xanthan gum.

**Mix** together the eggs, tomato paste and water in a separate bowl, add to the dry ingredients and combine to form a smooth mixture. Beat for 5 minutes, then stir in the remaining ingredients.

**Spoon** the mixture into the prepared tin, cover with a clean damp tea towel and leave in a warm place to rise for about 30 minutes until the mixture is near the top of the tin.

**Place** in a preheated oven, 180°C (350°F), Gas Mark 4, for about 45 minutes or it is until brown and sounds hollow when tapped on the bottom. Remove from the oven and transfer to a wire rack to cool.

**For apple & walnut bread**, make the dough as above, omitting the sun-dried tomato paste and replacing the Parmesan, olives and oregano with 1 large peeled and grated eating apple and 125 g (4 oz) chopped walnuts. Leave to prove and then bake as above.

# potato & thyme griddle scones

Preparation time **10 minutes**
Cooking time **15 minutes**
Makes **6**

250 g (8 oz) **potato**, peeled
  and cut into 1.5 cm (¾ inch)
  cubes
25 g (1 oz) **butter**, plus extra
  for cooking
50 g (2 oz) **rice flour**, plus
  extra for dusting
1 teaspoon **gluten-free
  baking powder**
1 teaspoon **thyme**, chopped,
  plus extra sprigs to garnish
  (optional)
2 tablespoons **buttermilk**
1 **egg**, beaten
**vegetable oil**, for brushing
**salt** also used to cook
  potatoes

**Cook** the potatoes in a saucepan of salted boiling water for 10 minutes or until tender. Drain well.

**Place** the potato and butter in a large bowl and mash together until smooth, then stir in the remaining ingredients together with a pinch of salt until combined. Bring the mixture together to form a ball.

**Turn** the dough out on to a surface lightly dusted with rice flour, roll into a round about 5 mm (¼ inch) thick and cut into 6 triangles.

**Brush** a griddle or nonstick frying pan with a little oil and add a knob of butter, then cook the scones for 2–3 minutes on each side until golden. Serve warm with butter and cheese, garnished with sprigs of thyme if liked.

**For cheesy potato, garlic & chive cakes**, stir 75 g (3 oz) crumbled Cheshire cheese into the potato mixture together with 1 crushed garlic clove and 1 teaspoon chopped chives in place of the thyme. Form into 6 rounds about 5mm (¼ inch) thick and cook as above.

# garlic & caramelized onion bhajis

Preparation **10 minutes**,
  plus standing
Cooking time **15 minutes**
Serves **6**

2 tablespoons **olive oil**
1 **onion**, sliced
2 **garlic cloves**, sliced
1 teaspoon **cumin seeds**
2 tablespoons chopped
  **coriander**
200 g (7 oz) **chickpea flour**
1 teaspoon **bicarbonate
  of soda**
½ teaspoon **salt**
250 ml (8 fl oz) **water**

**Heat** half the oil in a nonstick frying pan, add the onion, garlic and cumin and fry for 5–6 minutes until the onion is golden and softened. Stir in the coriander.

**Meanwhile,** mix together the flour, bicarbonate of soda, salt and water in a bowl and set aside for 10 minutes, then stir in the onion mixture.

**Heat** a little of the remaining oil in the frying pan, add spoonfuls of the onion mixture and fry for 2–3 minutes, turning halfway through cooking. Transfer to a serving plate and keep warm while frying the remainder of the mixture.

**For spicy spinach & onion bhajis**, make as above, adding 75 g (3 oz) cooked and well-squeezed chopped spinach to the frying pan with the coriander. Add ½ teaspoon dried chilli flakes to the flour mixture, then continue as above.

# corn & bacon muffins

Preparation time **10 minutes**
Cooking time **20–25 minutes**
Makes **12**

6 **streaky bacon rashers**,
  finely chopped
1 small **red onion**,
  finely chopped
200 g (7 oz) **frozen
  sweetcorn**
175 g (6 oz) **fine cornmeal**
125 g (4 oz) **gluten-free
  plain flour**
2 teaspoons **gluten-free
  baking powder**
50 g (2 oz) **Cheddar cheese**,
  grated
200 ml (7 fl oz) **milk**
2 **eggs**, beaten
3 tablespoons **vegetable oil**,
  plus extra for oiling

**Oil** a 12-hole muffin tray.

**Heat** a frying pan, add the bacon and onion and dry-fry for 3–4 minutes until the bacon is turning crisp.

**Cook** the sweetcorn in a saucepan of boiling water for 2 minutes to soften. Drain well.

**Mix** together the cornmeal, flour and baking powder in a bowl, then stir in the sweetcorn, cheese, bacon and onion. Mix together the milk, eggs and oil in a separate bowl, add to the dry ingredients and stir gently to combine.

**Pour** the mixture into the oiled holes and place in a preheated oven, 220°C (425°F), Gas Mark 7, for 15–20 minutes until golden and just firm to the touch. Remove from the oven and transfer to a wire rack to cool.

**For cheese & corn muffins**, omit the bacon and fry the onion in 1 tablespoon olive oil. Continue as above, adding an extra 25 g (1 oz) Cheddar cheese to the dry ingredients and 1 teaspoon smoked paprika and season well. Bake as above.

# pizza scrolls

Preparation time **25 minutes**, plus proving
Cooking time **12–15 minutes**
Makes **8**

2 x 7 g (¼ oz) sachets **fast-action dried yeast**
1 teaspoon **caster sugar**
250 ml (8 fl oz) **milk**, warmed
175 g (6 oz) **rice flour**, plus extra for dusting
125 g (4 oz) **potato flour**
1 teaspoon **gluten-free baking powder**
1 teaspoon **xanthan gum**
pinch of **salt**
1 tablespoon **sunflower oil**, plus extra for oiling
1 **egg**, beaten

**Filling**
4 tablespoons **passata**
200 g (7 oz) mixed **mozzarella** and **Cheddar cheese**, grated
75 g (3 oz) **wafer-thin ham**, shredded
handful of **basil**, chopped

**Put** the yeast, sugar and milk in a bowl and set aside for about 10 minutes until frothy. Stir together the flours, baking powder, xanthan gum and salt in a large bowl.

**Mix** together the oil and egg in a separate bowl, stir into the yeast mixture and add this to the dry ingredients. Combine to form a soft dough.

**Turn** the dough out on to a surface lightly dusted with rice flour and knead for 5 minutes, adding a little rice flour if the mixture becomes sticky. Place in a lightly oiled bowl, cover with a clean damp tea towel and leave in a warm place to rise for 40 minutes or until well risen.

**Roll** the dough out on the floured surface to a rectangle approximately 30 x 25 cm (12 x 10 inches), spread with the passata, then sprinkle over the remaining filling ingredients. Roll the pizza up from one long edge, then slice into 8 pieces.

**Place** the rolled-up pizza scrolls side by side on a lightly oiled heavy baking sheet or tin. They should be pushed up against each other so that the sides are touching. Place in a preheated oven, 220°C (425°F), Gas Mark 7, for 12–15 minutes until golden. Remove from the oven and serve warm.

**For olive & artichoke pizza scrolls**, make and roll out the dough as above. For the filling, spread over 2 tablespoons olive tapenade or sun-dried tomato paste. Scatter over 6 drained and thinly sliced bottled artichoke hearts, 150 g (5 oz) roughly chopped mozzarella cheese and 6 drained and sliced sun-dried tomatoes. in oil. Roll up and bake as above.

# spicy fruit & seed bread

Preparation time **10 minutes**,
plus proving
Cooking time **20–25 minutes**
Makes **1 x 500 g (1 lb) loaf**

150 g (5 oz) **chickpea flour**
150 g (5 oz) **gluten-free flour**
2 teaspoons **fast-action
dried yeast**
1 teaspoon **salt**
1 teaspoon **caster sugar**
1 tablespoon **black onion
seeds**
1 tablespoon **cumin seeds**
2 teaspoons **ground
coriander**
¼ teaspoon **dried chilli flakes**
50 g (2 oz) **dried mango** or
**pear**, chopped
2 tablespoons **groundnut oil**,
plus extra for oiling
200 ml (7 fl oz) **hand-hot
water**

**Grease** a 500 g (1 lb) loaf tin.

**Place** the flours, yeast, salt, sugar, spices and dried fruit in a bowl and stir to combine. Mix together the oil and water in a separate bowl, add to the dry ingredients and combine to form a stiff dough.

**Spoon** the mixture into the prepared tin, cover with a clean damp tea towel and leave in a warm place to rise for about 45 minutes or until the mixture is slightly above the top of the tin.

**Place** in a preheated oven, 200°C (400°F), Gas Mark 6, for 20–25 minutes until firm to the touch. Remove from the oven and transfer to a wire rack to cool. Serve cut into slices, spread with butter if liked.

### For toasted fruity bread with blackberries & plums,

heat 25 g (1 oz) butter in a nonstick saucepan, add 4 halved amd stoned plums and fry over a gentle heat until slightly softened. Stir in 125 g (4 oz) blackberries and 1 tablespoon caster sugar and cook for a further 1–2 minutes until the sugar has dissolved and the blackberries are beginning to release their juices. Meanwhile, toast 4 slices of Spicy Fruit & Seed Bread (see above) and butter lightly. Serve the fruit on the toast.

# desserts

# hazelnut meringue stack

Preparation time **10 minutes**, plus cooling
Cooking time **45 minutes**
Serves **8**

4 **egg whites**
250 g (8 oz) **caster sugar**
1 teaspoon **white wine vinegar**
100 g (3½ oz) **blanched hazelnuts**, toasted and roughly chopped
200 ml (7 fl oz) **double cream**
275 g (9 oz) **raspberries**
**cocoa powder**, for dusting

**Line** 3 baking sheets with nonstick baking paper.

**Whisk** the egg whites in a large clean bowl until they form stiff peaks. Add the sugar a spoonful at a time and continue to whisk until thick and glossy. Fold in the vinegar with a large metal spoon.

**Fold** half the hazelnuts into the mixture, then divide it between the prepared sheets, spooning the meringue into 3 rounds roughly 18 cm (7 inches) in diameter.

**Place** in a preheated oven, 150°C (300°F), Gas Mark 2, for 45 minutes, then switch off the oven and leave the meringue to cool.

**Whip** the cream in a bowl until it forms soft peaks, spoon the cream over 2 of the meringues and top each with the raspberries and remaining nuts, reserving a few raspberries for decoration.

**Stack** the meringues with the plain one on top, then dust with a little cocoa powder and decorate with the remaining raspberries. Serve on the same day or chill for up to 2 days.

**For banana, chocolate & fudge meringue**, make the meringues as above. Fold 2 chopped bananas into the whipped cream with 100 g (3½ oz) grated dark, plain chocolate and 100 g (3½ oz) chopped fudge pieces. Sandwich the meringues together with the whipped cream mixture as above, and decorate with gluten-free plain, dark chocolate shavings or curls.

# pear, apple & cinnamon crumble

Preparation time **10 minutes**
Cooking time **30–35 minutes**
Serves **4**

750 g (1½ lb) **pears**, peeled, cored and sliced
500 g (1 lb) **cooking apples**, peeled, cored and sliced
2 tablespoons **soft light brown sugar**
1 teaspoon **ground cinnamon**
4 tablespoons **apple juice**

**Topping**
200 g (7 oz) **rice flour**
100 g (3½ oz) **butter**, cubed
100 g (3½ oz) **soft light brown sugar**
25 g (1 oz) **flaked almonds**
25 g (1 oz) **blanched hazelnuts**, roughly chopped

**Put** the pears and apples in a large saucepan with the sugar, cinnamon and apple juice. Cover and cook gently, stirring occasionally, for about 10 minutes or until the fruit is just tender. Transfer to an ovenproof dish.

**Make** the topping. Place the flour and butter in a food processor and whizz until the mixture resembles fine breadcrumbs. Alternatively, place the flour in a large bowl, add the butter and rub in with the fingertips until the mixture resembles fine breadcrumbs. Stir in the sugar and nuts, then sprinkle over the fruit and press down gently.

**Place** in a preheated oven, 200°C (400°F), Gas Mark 6, for 20–25 minutes until golden and bubbling. Serve with crème fraîche or cream.

**For rhubarb & ginger crumble**, cut 1 kg (2 lb) rhubarb into chunks and put in an ovenproof dish with 2 tablespoons water and 6 tablespoons caster sugar. Place in a preheated oven, 200°C (400°F), Gas Mark 6, for 15 minutes, then stir in 1 teaspoon ground ginger. Make the topping as above, adding 100 g (3½ oz) finely chopped marzipan. Sprinkle over the rhubarb and bake in the oven as above.

# lemony cheesecake

Preparation time **10 minutes**,
  plus chilling
Serves **6**

125 g (4 oz) **gluten-free plain
  or ginger biscuits**, crushed
50 g (2 oz) **butter**, melted
250 g (8 oz) **mascarpone
  cheese**
grated rind and juice of
  **2 lemons**
150 ml (¼ pint) **double cream**
100 g (3½ oz) **icing sugar**,
  sifted

**To decorate**
**blueberries** and **raspberries**
**lemon rind curls**

**Mix** together the crushed biscuits and melted butter in a bowl, then press into the base and up the side of a 20 cm (8 inch) fluted loose-bottomed flan tin. Chill until firm.

**Beat** together the mascarpone, lemon rind and juice, double cream and icing sugar in a large bowl until thick, then spoon over the biscuit base. Chill for at least 30 minutes until firm.

**Decorate** with blueberries, raspberries and lemon rind curls, when ready to serve.

**For lemon & raspberry swirl cheesecake**, make the biscuit base and mascarpone mixture as above. Whizz together 200 g (7 oz) raspberries and 1 tablespoon icing sugar in a food processor or blender and gently fold into the mascarpone mixture. Spoon on to the biscuit base and chill until firm. Decorate with a few extra raspberries and serve.

# chocolate profiteroles

Preparation time **10 minutes**
Cooking time **30 minutes**
Makes **about 20**

150 ml (¼ pint) **water**
50 g (2 oz) **butter**, plus extra
for greasing
60 g (2¼ oz) **rice flour**
1 teaspoon **gluten-free
baking powder**
½ teaspoon **bicarbonate
of soda**
1 teaspoon **caster sugar**
2 **eggs**, beaten

**Chocolate sauce**
200 g (7 oz) **gluten-free plain
dark chocolate**, broken
into pieces
100 ml (3½ oz) **double cream**

**Cream filling**
200 ml (7 oz) **double cream**
1 tablespoon **icing sugar**

**Put** the water and butter in a saucepan and bring to the boil. Sift together the flour, baking powder, sugar and bicarbonate of soda into a bowl, then quickly tip into the pan and beat with a hand-held electric whisk. Gradually beat in the eggs until glossy, then spoon the mixture into a piping bag with a plain nozzle and pipe small mounds on to 2 lightly greased and dampened baking sheets.

**Place** in a preheated oven, 200°C (400°F), Gas Mark 6, for 10 minutes, then increase the temperature to 220°C (425°F), Gas Mark 7, and cook for a further 12–15 minutes until crisp and golden. Remove from the oven, pierce a hole in the side of each of the profiteroles and transfer to a wire rack to cool.

**Make** the chocolate sauce. Place the chocolate and cream in a heatproof bowl over a saucepan of simmering water and leave until melted. Stir together and leave to cool a little.

**Whip** the cream with the icing sugar in a bowl until it forms soft peaks and use to fill each bun. Pile the buns on to a serving dish, then pour over the chocolate sauce.

**For coffee profiteroles**, make and bake the profiteroles then leave to cool as above. Mix 2 teaspoons instant coffee with 2 teaspoons boiling water. Leave to cool. Stir in 100 g (3½ oz) mascarpone cheese with 100 ml (3½ oz) whipped cream and 1 tablespoon icing sugar. Use to fill the cooled profiteroles.

# easy banoffee pies

Preparation time **5 minutes**
Serves **4**

6 **gluten-free chocolate biscuits**, roughly crushed

400 g (13 oz) can **gluten-free caramel**

2 **bananas**, sliced

150 ml (¼ pint) **extra-thick double cream**

50 g (2 oz) **gluten-free plain dark chocolate**, shaved or grated

**Divide** the crushed biscuits between 4 tall glasses.

**Spoon** the caramel into each glass, then scatter over the banana slices.

**Top** with the cream and decorate with the chocolate. Serve immediately.

**For fudge sundaes,** place 2 scoops of gluten-free vanilla ice cream in each of 4 tall glasses. Mix together 100 g (3½ oz) melted gluten-free milk chocolate and half a 400 g (13 oz) can caramel in a bowl. Spoon the fudge over the ice cream, then scatter over a handful of chopped toasted hazelnuts and 1 sliced banana. Serve immediately.

# berry meringue mess

Preparation time **10 minutes**, plus cooling

Cooking time **1 hour**

Serves **6**

3 **egg whites**

250 g (8 oz) **caster sugar**

1 teaspoon **white wine vinegar**

300 ml (½ pint) **double cream**

200 g (7 oz) **raspberries**, plus extra, left whole, to decorate

200 g (7 oz) **strawberries**, hulled and quartered, plus extra, left whole and unhulled, to decorate

2 tablespoons **icing sugar**

2 tablespoons **cream liqueur**

**Line** 2 large baking sheets with nonstick baking paper.

**Whisk** the egg whites in a large clean bowl until they form stiff peaks. Add the sugar a spoonful at a time and continue to whisk until thick and glossy. Fold in the vinegar with a large metal spoon.

**Spoon** or pipe 12 meringues on to the prepared baking sheets. Place in a preheated oven, 150°C (300°F), Gas Mark 2, for 1 hour, then switch off the oven and leave the meringues to cool completely. When cool, roughly crush the meringues.

**Whip** the cream in a large bowl until it forms soft peaks. Roughly crush together the raspberries and strawberries and stir into the cream. Fold in the crushed meringues, icing sugar and cream liqueur. Spoon into 6 tall glasses, decorate with extra whole berries, and serve immediately.

**For mango & passion fruit mess**, make the meringues as above and roughly crush. Whip the cream with 2 tablespoons icing sugar in a large bowl until it forms soft peaks. Peel and stone 1 large mango and purée half the flesh in a food processor or blender. Chop the remaining mango flesh and stir all the mango into the cream mixture with the scooped flesh of 2 passion fruit. Fold in the crushed meringues and serve immediately.

# sticky toffee pudding

Preparation time **10 minutes**,
plus soaking
Cooking time **25–30 minutes**
Serves **8**

125 g (4 oz) **dried dates**,
stoned and chopped
200 ml (7 fl oz) **boiling water**
1 teaspoon **bicarbonate**
**of soda**
50 g (2 oz) **butter**, softened,
plus extra for greasing
50 g (2 oz) **soft light**
**brown sugar**
2 **eggs**, beaten
125 g (4 oz) **rice flour**
1 teaspoon **gluten-free**
**baking powder**

**To serve**
handful of chopped
**pecan nuts**
**thick cream**

**Toffee sauce**
200 g (7 oz) **butter**
300 g (10 oz) **soft light**
**brown sugar**
200 ml (7 fl oz) **double cream**

**Put** the dates in a heatproof bowl, pour over the boiling water and stir in the bicarbonate of soda. Leave to soak for 10 minutes.

**Grease** and line a 20 cm (8 inch) square cake tin.

**Beat** together the butter, sugar, eggs, flour, baking powder and soaked dates and their frothy liquid in a bowl. Pour into the prepared tin. Place in a preheated oven, 180°C (350°F), Gas Mark 4, for 25–30 minutes until firm to the touch.

**Place** all the sauce ingredients in a saucepan while the pudding cooking, and heat through until the sugar has dissolved. Cut the sponge into 8 pieces and serve warm in bowls topped with some thick cream, the toffee sauce and a scattering of pecan nuts.

**For sticky ginger loaf cake**, make the sponge mixture as above, adding 1 ½ teaspoons ground ginger. Pour into a 900 g (2 lb) greased and lined loaf tin and bake in the oven as above. Heat 25 g (1 oz) butter, 4 tablespoons soft light brown sugar and 2 tablespoons double cream in a small saucepan until the sugar has dissolved, then boil for 3 minutes. Leave the cake to cool slightly, then remove from the tin, peel away the lining paper and set on a serving plate. Pour over the sauce, scatter over a handful of chopped walnuts and serve.

# baked pears with marzipan

Preparation time **10 minutes**
Cooking time **25–30 minutes**
Serves **4**

4 **pears**, peeled, keeping
   the pears whole
juice of ½ **lemon**
50 g (2 oz) **marzipan**, grated
   or finely chopped
1 tablespoon **sultanas**
4 tablespoons **apple juice**
2 tablespoons **runny honey**
2 tablespoons **flaked
   almonds**, toasted

**Core** the pears from the bases, leaving the stalks in place, and coat with the lemon juice. Mix together the marzipan and sultanas in a bowl, then spoon the mixture into the cored cavity of the pears. Stand the stuffed pears in a small ovenproof dish.

**Spoon** over the apple juice, then drizzle over the honey and place in a preheated oven, 180°C (350°F), Gas Mark 4, for 25–30 minutes until tender.

**Remove** from the oven and scatter over the almonds. Serve with whipped cream or custard.

**For amaretti-stuffed pears**, prepare the pears as above. Mix together 4 stoned chopped apricots, 4 crushed amaretti biscuits, the juice of ½ orange and 1 tablespoon runny honey or maple syrup. Blend in a food processor or blender, and spoon into the pear cavities. Stand the stuffed pears in a small ovenproof dish and bake in the oven as above until tender.

# perfect pecan pies

Preparation time **15 minutes**,
  plus chilling
Cooking time **20–25 minutes**
Makes **8**

75 g (3 oz) **brown rice flour**,
  plus extra for dusting
50 g (2 oz) **chickpea flour**
75 g (3 oz) **polenta**
1 teaspoon **xanthan gum**
125 g (4 oz) **butter**, cubed
2 tablespoons **caster sugar**
1 **egg**, beaten

**Filling**
100 g (3½ oz) **soft light
  brown sugar**
150 g (5 oz) **butter**
125 g (4 oz) **honey**
175 g (6 oz) **pecan nut
  halves**, half roughly chopped
2 **eggs**, beaten

**Grease** and line 8 individual 11.5 cm (4½ inch) pie tins. Place the flours, polenta, xanthan gum and butter in a food processor and whizz until the mixture resembles fine breadcrumbs. Alternatively, mix together the flours, polenta and xanthan gum in a large bowl. Add the butter and rub in with the fingertips until the mixture resembles fine breadcrumbs. Stir in the sugar.

**Add** the egg and enough cold water to form a dough. Knead for a couple of minutes, then wrap in clingfilm and chill for about 1 hour.

**Place** the sugar, butter and honey for the filling in a saucepan and heat until the sugar has dissolved. Leave to cool for 10 minutes.

**Turn** the dough out on a surface lightly dusted with rice flour and knead to soften it a little. Divide the dough into 8, then roll each piece out to a thickness of 2.5 mm (⅛ inch) and use to line the pie tins. Stir the chopped pecans and eggs into the filling mixture and pour into the pastry-lined tins. Arrange the pecan halves on top.

**Place** in a preheated oven, 200°C (400°F), Gas Mark 6, for 15–20 minutes until the filling is firm. Remove from the oven and leave to cool in the tins.

**For homemade vanilla ice cream**, to serve as an accompaniment, whip 300 ml (½ pint) double cream with 2 tablespoons caster sugar in a bowl until it forms soft peaks. Fold in a 400 g (13 oz) can ready-made gluten-free custard and 1 teaspoon vanilla extract. Pour into a freezerproof container and freeze for 2 hours, then stir with a fork. Put back in the freezer for at least 6 hours, or until solid, then serve with the pecan pies.

# chocolate & chestnut roulade

Preparation time **15 minutes**
Cooking time **20 minutes**
Serves **8**

**butter**, for greasing
6 **eggs**, separated
125 g (4 oz) **caster sugar**
2 tablespoons **cocoa powder**
**icing sugar**, for dusting

**Filling**
150 ml (¼ pint) **double cream**
100 g (3½ oz) **chestnut**
   **purée** or **sweetened**
   **chestnut spread**

**Grease** and line a 29 x 18 cm (11½ x 7 inch) Swiss roll tin.

**Whisk** the egg whites in a large clean bowl until they form soft peaks. Whisk together the egg yolks and sugar in a separate bowl until thick and pale. Fold the cocoa powder and egg whites into the egg yolk mixture.

**Spoon** the mixture into the prepared tin and place in a preheated oven, 180°C (350°F), Gas Mark 4, for 20 minutes. Remove from the oven and cool in the tin.

**Turn** the cooled sponge out on to a piece of greaseproof paper dusted with icing sugar.

**Whip** the cream for the filling in a large clean bowl until it forms soft peaks. Fold the chestnut purée or sweetened chestnut spread into the cream, then smooth the filling over the sponge.

**Using** the greaseproof paper to help you, carefully roll up the roulade from one short end and lift it gently on to its serving dish. (Don't worry if it cracks: it won't detract from its appearance or taste.) Dust with icing sugar. Chill until needed and eat on the day it is made.

**For chocolate & black cherry roulade**, make the sponge as above. To make the filling, omit the chestnut purée or spread and replace with a 400 g (13 oz) can drained black cherries. Spread over the sponge, roll up and dust with icing sugar.

# christmas pudding

Preparation time **20 minutes**,
plus overnight soaking
Cooking time **8 hours**
Serves **6–8**

150 g (5 oz) **gluten-free suet**
2 tablespoons **rice flour**
200 g (7 oz) **gluten-free fresh breadcrumbs**
200 g (7 oz) **soft dark brown sugar**
500 g (1 lb) mixed **sultanas, raisins** and **currants**
100 g (3½ oz) **ready-to-eat dried apricots**, chopped
2 teaspoons **mixed spice**
1 **apple**, grated
2 large **eggs**
4 tablespoons **brandy**
4 tablespoons **apple juice**
grated rind of **1 orange**
**thick cream** to serve

**Mix** together all the ingredients in a large bowl, cover and leave to soak for 24 hours.

**Spoon** the mixture into a 1.2 litre (2 pint) pudding basin, cover with a piece of nonstick baking paper that has been folded with a pleat and secure with string, then cover with foil.

**Steam** the pudding for about 6 hours, keeping the water topped up in the saucepan so that it does not dry out. When cooked, rewrap the pudding in nonstick baking paper and foil. Store in a cool place until Christmas time.

**When** ready to serve, steam the pudding for a further 2 hours as above. Serve hot with thick cream.

**For Christmas pudding ice cream**, whip 300 ml (½ pint) double cream in a bowl until it forms soft peaks. Stir in a 400 g (13 oz) can ready-made gluten-free custard, 200 g (7 oz) crumbled Christmas Pudding (see above) and 2 tablespoons brandy. Pour into a freezerproof container and freeze for 2 hours, then stir with a fork. Put back in the freezer for at least 6 hours, or until solid, then serve.

# traditional cakes & bakes

# strawberry scones

Preparation time **10 minutes**
Cooking time **12 minutes**
Makes **8**

175 g (6 oz) **rice flour**, plus
 extra for dusting
75 g (3 oz) **potato flour**
1 teaspoon **xanthan gum**
1 teaspoon **gluten-free
 baking powder**
1 teaspoon **bicarbonate
 of soda**
75 g (3 oz) **butter**, cubed
40 g (1½ oz) **caster sugar**
1 large **egg**, beaten
3 tablespoons **buttermilk**,
 plus extra for brushing

**Filling**
150 ml (¼ pint) **double cream**
250 g (8 oz) **strawberries**,
 hulled and lightly crushed

**Place** the flours, xanthan gum, baking powder, bicarbonate of soda and butter in a food processor and whizz until the mixture resembles fine breadcrumbs. Alternatively, mix together the flours, xanthan gum, baking powder and bicarbonate of soda in a large bowl. Add the butter and rub in with the fingertips until the mixture resembles fine breadcrumbs. Stir in the sugar.

**Mix** together the egg and buttermilk in a separate bowl, add to the dry ingredients and mix to a soft dough.

**Turn** the dough out on a surface lightly dusted with rice flour, gently press out to a thickness of 2.5 cm (1 inch) and use a 5 cm (2 inch) cutter to stamp out 8 scones, rerolling the trimmings as necessary.

**Put** on a baking sheet lightly dusted with rice flour, brush with a little buttermilk and place in a preheated oven, 220°C (425°F), Gas Mark 7, for about 12 minutes until risen and golden. Remove from the oven and transfer to a wire rack to cool.

**Whip** the cream in a bowl until it forms fairly firm peaks and fold in the strawberries. Split the scones in half and fill with the strawberry cream.

**For fruit scones**, add 100 g (3½ oz) sultanas and ½ teaspoon ground cinnamon to the ingredients in the food processor, before processing or to the dry ingredients before rubbing in the butter. Continue as above. Serve the scones warm with butter and jam, if liked.

# boozy christmas cake

Preparation time **20 minutes**, plus soaking

Cooking time **4–4½ hours**

Serves **12–14**

800 g (1 lb 10 oz) mixed **sultanas, raisins** and **currants**

100 g (3½ oz) **ready-to-eat dried apricots**, diced

100 g (3½ oz) **glacé cherries**, rinsed and halved

grated rind of 2 **oranges**

150 ml (¼ pint) **brandy**, plus extra to feed and decorate

225 g (7½ oz) **butter**, softened

225 g (7½ oz) **soft dark brown sugar**

1 tablespoon **black treacle**

225 g (7½ oz) **rice flour**

1 teaspoon **mixed spice**

4 **eggs**, beaten

50 g (2 oz) **blanched almonds**, cut into slivers

**To decorate**

3 tablespoons **apricot jam**

50 g (2 oz) each **pecan nuts, blanched almonds, glacé cherries** and ready-to-eat **dried apricots**

**Mix** together the dried fruit, glacé cherries and orange rind in a bowl and pour over the brandy. Stir well, cover and leave to soak for 24 hours.

**Grease** and line a 20 cm (8 inch) round deep cake tin. Wrap and tie a double thickness of brown paper or newspaper around the outside of the tin to come 5 cm (2 inches) above the rim.

**Beat** the butter and sugar together in a large bowl until light and fluffy. Mix in the treacle. Sift together the flour and spice, then fold into the creamed mixture alternately with a little of the eggs until all the flour and eggs are combined. Stir in the soaked fruit, plus any juices, and the almonds.

**Spoon** the mixture into the prepared tin, ensuring it is pressed right into the base. Cover with a piece of greaseproof paper with a small hole in the middle. Place in a preheated oven, 140°C (275°F), Gas Mark 1, for about 4–4½ hours or until a skewer inserted into the middle of the cake comes out clean. Remove from the oven, remove the paper and cool in the tin.

**Feed** the cake by piercing holes in the surface and drizzling with brandy. When cold, remove from the tin, wrap in foil and store in an airtight container for up to 2 months. Feed once a week until required.

**Place** the jam and 1 tablespoon brandy in a small saucepan over a low heat until melted. Halve the cherries and apricots, then stir into the pan with the nuts, until well coated. Spoon over the cake and leave to set.

# coconut & mango cake

Preparation time **10 minutes**
Cooking time **45–50 minutes**
Serves **12**

100 g (3½ oz) **butter**,
  softened, plus extra
  for greasing
100 g (3½ oz) **soft light
  brown sugar**
4 **eggs**, separated
400 ml (14 fl oz) **buttermilk**
200 g (7 oz) **polenta**
200 g (7 oz) **rice flour**
2 teaspoons **gluten-free
  baking powder**
50 g (2 oz) **coconut
  milk powder**
50 g (2 oz) **desiccated
  coconut**
1 **mango**, peeled, stoned
  and puréed

**Filling**
250 g (8 oz) **mascarpone
  cheese**
1 **mango**, peeled, stoned
  and finely chopped
2 tablespoons **icing sugar**

**Grease** and line a 23 cm (9 inch) round deep cake tin.

**Beat** together the butter and sugar in a large bowl until light and fluffy, then beat in the egg yolks, buttermilk, polenta, flour, baking powder, coconut milk powder and desiccated coconut.

**Whisk** the egg whites in a large clean bowl until they form soft peaks, then fold into the cake mixture with the puréed mango.

**Spoon** the mixture into the prepared tin and place in a preheated oven, 200°C (400°F), Gas Mark 6, for 45–50 minutes until golden and firm to the touch. Remove from the oven and transfer to a wire rack to cool.

**Slice** the cake in half horizontally, when cool. Beat together the filling ingredients in a bowl and use half to sandwich the cakes together. Smooth the remaining mixture over the top.

**For peach delight cake**, make the sponge as above, replacing the mango purée with 3 puréed canned peach halves. For the filling, beat together the mascarpone and icing sugar with 2 chopped canned peach halves. Sandwich the cakes together with half the filling mixture and top with the remainder as above.

# chocolate & rum cake

Preparation time **15 minutes**
Cooking time **20–25 minutes**
Serves **16**

150 g (5 oz) **gluten-free plain dark chocolate**, broken into pieces

grated rind and juice of **1 orange**

few drops of **rum essence** (optional)

150 g (5 oz) **unsalted butter**, softened, plus extra for greasing

150 g (5 oz) **caster sugar**

4 **eggs**, separated

150 g (5 oz) **ground almonds**

**Chocolate icing**

150 g (5 oz) **gluten-free plain dark chocolate**, broken into pieces

100 g (3½ oz) **unsalted butter**

**Grease** and line 2 x 20 cm (8 inch) sandwich cake tins.

**Place** the chocolate, orange rind and juice and rum essence, if using, in a heatproof bowl over a saucepan of simmering water and leave until melted.

**Beat** together the butter and all but 1 tablespoon of the sugar in a large bowl until light and fluffy. Beat in the egg yolks, one by one, then stir in the melted chocolate.

**Whisk** the egg whites in a large clean bowl until they form soft peaks. Add the remaining sugar and continue to whisk until stiff peaks form. Fold the egg whites into the chocolate mixture with the ground almonds.

**Spoon** the mixture into the prepared tins and place in a preheated oven, 180°C (350°F), Gas Mark 4, for 20–25 minutes until the sides are cooked but the centre is still a little unset. Remove from the oven, leave to cool for a few minutes in the tins, then turn out gently on to a wire rack to cool completely.

**Make** the icing. Melt the chocolate as above, then whisk in the butter, a tablespoon at a time, until melted. Remove from the heat and whisk occasionally until cool. If the icing is runny, chill until it firms up a little. Fill and ice the cooled cake with the chocolate mixture.

**For crystallized violet petals**, to decorate the cake whisk 1 egg white with 1 teaspoon water in a bowl until frothy. Place clean violet petals on a plate, then, using a clean fine paintbrush, gently brush each side of the petals with the egg white. Dust with caster sugar and leave to dry overnight.

# victoria sandwich cake

Preparation time **10 minutes**
Cooking time **20 minutes**
Serves **12**

175 g (6 oz) **butter**, softened,
  plus extra for greasing
175 g (6 oz) **caster sugar**
175 g (6 oz) **brown rice flour**,
  plus extra for dusting
3 **eggs**
1 tablespoon **gluten-free
  baking powder**
few drops of **vanilla extract**
1 tablespoon **milk**

**To decorate**
4 tablespoons **raspberry jam**
**icing sugar**

**Grease** and flour 2 x 18 cm (7 inch) round cake tins. Place all the cake ingredients in a food processor and whizz until smooth or beat together in a large bowl until light and fluffy.

**Spoon** the mixture into the prepared tins and place in a preheated oven, 200°C (400°F), Gas Mark 6, for about 20 minutes until risen and golden. Remove from the oven and transfer to a wire rack to cool.

**Sandwich** the cooled cakes together with the jam and dust with icing sugar.

**For chocolate cake**, make the cakes as above, replacing 1 tablespoon of the rice flour with cocoa powder. For the chocolate icing, dissolve 2 tablespoons cocoa powder in 2 tablespoons boiling water and leave to cool. Beat together 375 g (12 oz) icing sugar and 175 g (6 oz) softened butter until light and fluffy, then beat in the cocoa mixture. Use to sandwich together and cover the cooled cakes.

# lemon drizzle loaf

Preparation time **15 minutes**
Cooking time **35–40 minutes**
Serves **12**

250 g (8 oz) **butter**, softened,
  plus extra for greasing
250 g (8 oz) **caster sugar**
250 g (8 oz) **brown rice flour**
2 teaspoons **gluten-free
  baking powder**
4 **eggs**, beaten
grated rind and juice of
  1 **lemon**
**lemon rind twist**, to decorate
  (optional)

**Lemon drizzle**
grated rind and juice of 2
  **lemons**
100 g (3½ oz) **granulated
  sugar**

**Grease** and line a 900 g (2 lb) loaf tin.

**Place** all the cake ingredients in a food processor and whizz until smooth or beat together in a large bowl until light and fluffy.

**Spoon** the mixture into the prepared tin and place in a preheated oven, 180°C (350°F), Gas Mark 4, for 35–40 minutes until golden and firm to the touch. Remove from the oven and transfer to a wire rack.

**Prick** holes all over the sponge with a cocktail stick. Mix together the drizzle ingredients in a bowl, then drizzle the liquid over the warm loaf. Leave until completely cold. Decorate with a twist of lemon rind, if liked.

**For orange & apricot loaf**, place 125 g (4 oz) chopped ready-to-eat dried apricots and the juice of 1 orange in a saucepan and simmer for 5 minutes, then leave to cool. Meanwhile, make the sponge mixture as above, replacing the lemon rind and juice with the grated rind of 1 orange. Stir in the soaked apricots and any juice, spoon into the prepared tin and bake as above. Mix the grated rind and juice of 1 large orange and 100 g (3½ oz) granulated sugar together and drizzle over the top of the warm loaf as above.

# tropical fruit cake

Preparation time **15 minutes**, plus soaking
Cooking time **1½–2 hours**
Serves **14**

grated rind and juice of
  2 **oranges**
grated rind of 1 **lemon**
300 g (10 oz) **raisins**
500 g (1 lb) **dried tropical fruit**, chopped
1 tablespoon **crystallized ginger**, chopped
3 tablespoons **brandy**
250 g (8 oz) **butter**, softened, plus extra for greasing
250 g (8 oz) **soft light brown sugar**
100 g (3½ oz) **soya flour**
125 g (4 oz) **rice flour**
1 teaspoon **mixed spice**
75 g (3 oz) **ground almonds**
4 **eggs**, beaten

**To decorate**
300 g (10 oz) **dried fruit** or **nuts**
2 tablespoons **apricot jam**, sieved and warmed

**Mix** together the orange rind and juice, lemon rind, raisins, dried fruit and ginger in a bowl then pour over the brandy. Stir well, cover and leave to soak overnight.

**Grease** and line an 18 cm (7 inch) square or a 20 cm (8 inch) round deep cake tin. Wrap and tie a double thickness of brown paper or newspaper around the outside of the tin to come 5 cm (2 inches) above the rim.

**Beat** together the butter and sugar in a bowl until light and fluffy. Sift together the flours and spice into a separate bowl and stir in the ground almonds. Gradually add the eggs to the creamed mixture, adding a little flour mixture if it begins to curdle. Fold in the remaining flour mixture and the soaked fruit and any juice.

**Spoon** the mixture into the prepared tin and place in a preheated oven, 160°C (325°F), Gas Mark 3, for 1½–2 hours or until a skewer inserted into the middle of the cake comes out clean. Remove from the oven, remove the paper and transfer to a wire rack to cool.

**Decorate** the cooled cake with the dried fruit or nuts and glaze with the apricot jam.

**For traditionally iced fruit cake**, make the marzipan by mixing together 375 g (12 oz) icing sugar, 375 g (12 oz) ground almonds, 2 lightly beaten egg whites and 1 teaspoon almond extract in a bowl. Add a little extra icing sugar if it is too sticky. Form into a ball, wrap in clingfilm and chill overnight. Make and bake the cake as above. Once cooled, cover with the rolled out marzipan, then top with royal icing and decorate as liked.

# beetroot speckled cake

Preparation time **15 minutes**
Cooking time **45–50 minutes**
Serves **10**

200 g (7 oz) **butter,** melted,
  plus extra for greasing
200 g (7 oz) **soft light brown
  sugar**
200 g (7 oz) **raw beetroot,**
  peeled and grated
150 g (5 oz) **whole mixed
  nuts**, toasted and chopped
3 **eggs**, separated
1 teaspoon **gluten-free
  baking powder**
½ teaspoon **ground
  cinnamon**
grated rind and juice of
  1 **orange**
200 g (7 oz) **rice flour**
3 tablespoons **ground
  almonds**

**To decorate**
200 g (7 oz) **cream cheese**
1 tablespoon **icing sugar**
150 g (5 oz) **whole
  mixed nuts**

**Grease** a 20 cm (8 inch) round deep cake tin.

**Whisk** together the melted butter and sugar in a large bowl until pale. Stir in the beetroot, two-thirds of the nuts and the egg yolks.

**Stir** together the baking powder, cinnamon, orange rind and juice, flour and ground almonds in a separate bowl. Add to the beetroot mixture and beat until smooth.

**Whisk** the egg whites in a large clean bowl until they form soft peaks, then fold into the beetroot mixture.

**Spoon** the mixture into the prepared tin and place in a preheated oven, 200°C (400°F), Gas Mark 6, for 45–50 minutes until firm to the touch. Remove from the oven and transfer to a wire rack to cool.

**Beat** together the cream cheese and icing sugar in a bowl, then smooth the icing over the top of the cooled cake. Decorate with the whole nuts.

**For chocolate beetroot cake**, make the cake mixture as above and fold in 100 g (3½ oz) chopped gluten-free plain dark chocolate. Bake as above and leave to cool. Top the cake with grated gluten-free plain dark chocolate.

# small cakes, biscuits & tray bakes

# chocolate caramel shortbread

Preparation time **20 minutes**,
  plus chilling
Cooking time **15 minutes**
Makes **15**

100 g (3½ oz) **butter**,
  softened, plus extra
  for greasing
50 g (2 oz) **caster sugar**
100 g (3½ oz) **brown
  rice flour**
100 g (3½ oz) **cornflour**

**Caramel**
100 g (3½ oz) **butter**
50 g (2 oz) **soft light
  brown sugar**
400 g (13 oz) **can
  condensed milk**

**Topping**
100 g (3½ oz) **gluten-free
  white chocolate**
100 g (3½ oz) **gluten-free
  plain dark chocolate**

**Grease** a 28 x 18 cm (11 x 7 inch) baking tin.

**Beat** together the butter and sugar in a large bowl until light and fluffy, then stir in the flours until well combined.

**Press** the shortbread into the prepared tin and place in a preheated oven, 200°C (400°F), Gas Mark 6, for 10–12 minutes until golden.

**Place** the caramel ingredients in a heavy-based saucepan and heat over a low heat until the sugar has dissolved, then cook for 5 minutes, stirring continuously. Remove from the heat and leave to cool a little.

**Remove** the shortbread base from the oven, then pour the caramel over and leave to cool and set.

**Place** the white and dark chocolate in separate heatproof bowls over saucepans of simmering water and leave until melted. When the caramel is firm, spoon alternate spoonfuls of the white and dark chocolate over the caramel, tap the tin on the work surface so that the different chocolates join, then use a knife to make swirls in the chocolate.

**Chill** until set, then cut the shortbread into 15 squares.

**For white chocolate & orange shortbread**, make the shortbread base as above, adding the grated rind of 1 orange and 100 g (3½ oz) gluten-free white chocolate chips to the mixture. Press into the prepared tin and bake in the oven as above. Leave to cool, then cut into 15 pieces.

# bakewell slice

Preparation time **20 minutes**
Cooking time **20–25 minutes**
Makes **12**

75 g (3 oz) **polenta**
75 g (3 oz) **brown rice flour**
½ teaspoon **xanthan gum**
100 g (3½ oz) **butter**, cubed,
plus extra for greasing
grated rind of 1 **lemon**
1 tablespoon **golden
caster sugar**
1 **egg yolk**, beaten
4 tablespoons **raspberry jam**
50 g (2 oz) **flaked almonds**,
toasted

**Sponge**
2 **eggs**
125 g (4 oz) **caster sugar**
125 g (4 oz) **rice flour**
125 g (4 oz) **butter**, softened
50 g (2 oz) **ground almonds**
1 teaspoon **gluten-free
baking powder**

**Grease** a 28 x 18 cm (11 x 7 inch) deep baking tin.

**Place** the polenta, flour, xanthan gum, butter and sugar in a food processor and whizz until the mixture resembles fine breadcrumbs. Alternatively, mix together the polenta, flour and xanthan gum in a large bowl. Add the butter and rub in with the fingertips until the mixture resembles fine breadcrumbs. Stir in the lemon rind and sugar.

**Add** the egg yolk and enough cold water to form a dough. Press the pastry into the prepared tin and spread over the jam.

**Place** all the sponge ingredients in a food processor and whizz until smooth or beat together in a large bowl until light and fluffy.

**Spoon** the mixture into the baking tin and place in a preheated oven, 200°C (400°F), Gas Mark 6, for 20–25 minutes until just firm to the touch.

**Remove** from the oven and leave to cool in the tin. Scatter over the toasted almonds and cut into 12 slices.

**For chocolate sponge tart**, make the pastry as above and use to line the tin. Prick the pastry base with a fork and place in the preheated oven for 10 minutes. Make the sponge mixture as above, adding 25 g (1 oz) cocoa powder, the grated rind of 1 orange and 2 tablespoons milk. Spoon into the pastry case and bake in the oven as above.

# chewy nutty chocolate brownies

Preparation time **10 minutes**
Cooking time **30 minutes**
Makes **15**

75 g (3 oz) **gluten-free plain
dark chocolate**, broken
into pieces
100 g (3½ oz) **butter**, plus
extra for greasing
200 g (7 oz) **soft light
brown sugar**
2 **eggs**, beaten
few drops of **vanilla extract**
50 g (2 oz) **ground almonds**
25 g (1 oz) **brown rice flour**
150 g (5 oz) **mixed nuts**,
toasted and roughly chopped
**vanilla ice cream**, to serve

**Grease** and line a 28 x 18 cm (11 x 7 inch) baking tin.

**Place** the chocolate and butter in a large heatproof
bowl over a saucepan of simmering water and leave
until melted. Stir in all the remaining ingredients and
combine well.

**Pour** the mixture into the prepared tin and place in
a preheated oven, 180°C (350°F), Gas Mark 4, for
30 minutes until slightly springy in the centre.

**Remove** from the oven and leave to cool for 10
minutes in the tin, then cut into 15 squares. Serve
with a generous dollop of vanilla ice cream.

### For macadamia & white chocolate brownies,
omit the plain dark chocolate and melt the butter in
a large saucepan. Stir in 100 g (3½ oz) gluten-free
white chocolate, cut into chunks, with the remaining
ingredients, replacing the mixed nuts with 150 g
(5 oz) roughly chopped macadamia nuts. Pour into
the prepared tin and bake in the oven as above.

# pistachio & choc chip shortbread

Preparation time **10 minutes**
Cooking time **20 minutes**
Makes **12**

100 g (3½ oz) **butter**,
  softened, plus extra
  for greasing
50 g (2 oz) **caster sugar**
100 g (3½ oz) **rice flour**
100 g (3½ oz) **cornflour**
50 g (2 oz) **gluten-free plain
  dark chocolate drops** or
  **gluten-free plain dark
  chocolate**, chopped
50 g (2 oz) **pistachio nuts**,
  chopped
75 g (3 oz) **gluten-free plain
  dark chocolate**, melted,
  to decorate

**Grease** a 28 x 18 cm (11 x 7 inch) baking tin.

**Beat** together the butter and sugar in a large bowl until light and fluffy. Stir in the flours, chocolate drops or chopped chocolate and pistachios until well combined.

**Press** the mixture into the prepared tin and place in a preheated oven, 180°C (350°F), Gas Mark 4, for 20 minutes until golden.

**Remove** from the oven and mark into 12 triangles, then transfer to a wire rack to cool completely before removing from the tin. (It is sometimes easier to remove the shortbread from the tin once it has been chilled a little.) Drizzle with the melted chocolate. Leave to set, then separate into triangles.

**For macadamia & white chocolate brownies**, make the mixture as above, replacing the pistachios with 50 g (2 oz) chopped macadamia nuts and 50 g (2 oz) chopped gluten-free white chocolate. Continue as above.

# cherry crumble muffins

Preparation time **10 minutes**
Cooking time **20 minutes**
Makes **12**

250 g (8 oz) **brown rice flour**
1 teaspoon **bicarbonate of soda**
2 teaspoons **gluten-free baking powder**
125 g (4 oz) **golden caster sugar**
300 g (10 oz) can **black cherries**, drained
75 g (3 oz) **butter**, melted
2 **eggs**, beaten
150 ml (¼ pint) **buttermilk**

**Topping**
1 tablespoon **ground almonds**
1 tablespoon **soft light brown sugar**
1 tablespoon **brown rice flour**
15 g (½ oz) **butter**

**Line** a large 12-hole muffin tray with large muffin cases.

**Sift** together the flour, bicarbonate of soda and baking powder into a large bowl, then stir in the sugar.

**Mix** together the cherries, melted butter, eggs and buttermilk in a separate bowl, add to the dry ingredients and stir gently until just combined. Spoon the mixture into the muffin cases.

**Place** the topping ingredients in a food processor and whizz until the mixture resembles fine breadcrumbs. Alternatively, mix together the ground almonds, sugar and four in a bowl. Add the butter and rub in with the finegrtips until the mixture resembles fine breadcrumbs. Sprinkle over the muffin mixture.

**Place** in a preheated oven, 180°C (350°F), Gas Mark 4, for 20 minutes until golden and firm to the touch. Remove from the oven, transfer to a wire rack and leave to cool.

**For banana fudge muffins**, make the muffin mixture as above, replacing the cherries with 2 small chopped bananas and 100 g (3½ oz) chopped fudge. Instead of the crumble topping, place 1 banana chip and 1 small piece of fudge on top of each muffin, then bake in the oven as above.

# lemon & raspberry cupcakes

Preparation time **10 minutes**
Cooking time **12–15 minutes**
Makes **12**

150 g (5 oz) **butter**, softened
150 g (5 oz) **caster sugar**
75 g (3 oz) **rice flour**
75 g (3 oz) **cornflour**
1 tablespoon **gluten-free baking powder**
grated rind and juice of
   **1 lemon**
3 **eggs**, beaten
125 g (4 oz) **raspberries**
1 tablespoon **gluten-free lemon curd**

**Line** a large 12-hole muffin tray with large muffin cases.

**Whisk** together all the ingredients except the raspberries and the lemon curd in a large bowl. Fold in the raspberries.

**Spoon** half the sponge mixture into the muffin cases, dot over a little of the lemon curd, then add the remaining sponge mixture.

**Place** in a preheated oven, 200°C (400°F), Gas Mark 6, for 12–15 minutes until golden and firm to the touch. Remove from the oven, transfer to a wire rack and leave to cool.

**For citrusy muffins**, make the sponge mixture as above, adding the grated rind of 1 orange. Omit the raspberries and lemon curd and cook as above. Mix 150 g (5 oz) icing sugar and 1–2 teaspoons lemon juice in a bowl to make a fairly thick icing and drizzle over the cooled muffins. Decorate with gluten-free lemon and orange jelly sweets, if liked.

# lavender cupcakes

Preparation time **10 minutes**
Cooking time **13–20 minutes**
Makes **12**

1 tablespoon **milk**
1 teaspoon **lavender flowers**
(flowerheads only)
125 g (4 oz) **caster sugar**
100 g (3½ oz) **butter,**
softened
100 g (3½ oz) **rice flour**
1 tablespoon **chickpea flour**
2 **eggs**, beaten
2 tablespoons **ground
almonds**
1 teaspoon **gluten-free
baking powder**
1 teaspoon **xanthan gum**

**To decorate**
125 g (4 oz) **icing sugar**
12 small **lavender
flowerheads**

**Line** a 12-hole bun tin with paper cases.

**Place** the milk and lavender in a ramekin, cover with clingfilm and microwave on full power for 10 seconds, or place in a preheated oven, 180°C, (350°F), Gas Mark 4, for 5 minutes. Remove and leave for 10 minutes to allow the flavours to develop.

**Place** all the cake ingredients, including the lavender-infused milk, in a food processor and whizz until smooth or beat together in a large bowl.

**Spoon** the mixture into the paper cases and place in a preheated oven, 180°C (350°F) Gas Mark 4, for 12–15 minutes until golden and just firm to the touch. Remove from the oven and transfer to a wire rack to cool.

**Add** a few drops of water to the icing sugar – just enough to make a stiff icing. Smooth a little over each cupcake and decorate with a lavender flowerhead.

**For lavender orange cupcakes**, add the grated rind of 1 orange to the milk and lavender and continue to make the cupcake mixture as above. Bake and cool the cupcakes, as above, then use a little orange juice instead of water to make the icing, spread over the cakes and decorate with orange rind curls.

# fruity mango flapjacks

Preparation time **10 minutes**
Cooking time **35 minutes**
Makes **12**

100 g (3½ oz) **soft light brown sugar**
150 g (5 oz) **butter**, plus extra for greasing
2 tablespoons **golden syrup**
200 g (7 oz) **millet flakes**
2 tablespoons **mixed pumpkin** and **sunflower seeds**
75 g (3 oz) **dried mango**, roughly chopped

**Grease** a 28 x 18 cm (11 x 7 inch) baking tin.

**Place** the sugar, butter and syrup in a heavy-based saucepan and heat until melted, then stir in the remaining ingredients.

**Spoon** the mixture into the prepared tin, press down lightly and place in a preheated oven, 150°C (300°F), Gas Mark 2, for 30 minutes.

**Remove** from the oven and mark into 12 bars, then place on a wire rack to cool completely before removing from the tin and breaking into bars.

**For blueberry & hazelnut bars**, heat the sugar, butter and golden syrup until melted as above. Stir in the millet flakes with 125 g (4 oz) dried blueberries and 125 g (4 oz) chopped toasted hazelnuts. Spoon the mixture into the tin and bake as above.

# chocolate chip cookies

Preparation time **10 minutes**
Cooking time **10 minutes**
Makes **30**

75 g (3 oz) **butter**, softened,
   plus extra for greasing
100 g (3½ oz) **caster sugar**
75 g (3 oz) **soft light
   brown sugar**
1 **egg**, beaten
150 g (5 oz) **brown rice flour**,
   plus extra for dusting
½ teaspoon **bicarbonate
   of soda**
1 tablespoon **cocoa powder**
75 g (3 oz) **gluten-free plain
   dark chocolate chips**

**Grease** 3 baking sheets.

**Put** all the ingredients except the chocolate chips in a food processor and whizz until smooth or beat together in a large bowl. Stir in the chocolate chips, then bring the mixture together to form a ball.

**Turn** the dough out on a surface lightly dusted with rice flour and divide into 30 balls. Place on the prepared sheets, well spaced apart, pressing down gently with the back of a fork.

**Place** in a preheated oven, 180°C (350°F), Gas Mark 4, for 8–10 minutes. Remove from the oven, leave for a few minutes on the baking sheets to harden, then transfer to a wire rack to cool.

**For crunchy ginger cookies**, make the dough as above, replacing the cocoa powder and chocolate chips with 2 teaspoons ground ginger. Continue as above, sprinkling a little demerara sugar over the cookies once they have been pressed down with a fork. Bake in the oven as above.

# orange & polenta cookies

Preparation time **10 minutes**, plus chilling

Cooking time **8 minutes**

Makes **20**

75 g (3 oz) **polenta**
25 g (1 oz) **rice flour**
25 g (1 oz) **ground almonds**
½ teaspoon **gluten-free baking powder**
75 g (3 oz) **icing sugar**
50 g (2 oz) **butter,** cubed
1 **egg yolk**, beaten
grated rind of **1 orange**
25 g (1 oz) **flaked almonds**

**Line** 2 baking sheets with nonstick baking paper.

**Place** the polenta, flour, ground almonds, baking powder, icing sugar and butter in a food processor and whizz until the mixture resembles fine breadcrumbs. Alternatively, mix together the polenta, flour, ground almonds, baking powder and icing sugar in a large bowl. Add the butter and rub in with the fingertips until the mixture resembles fine breadcrumbs.

**Add** the egg yolk and orange rind and combine to form a firm dough. Wrap in clingfilm and chill for 30 minutes.

**Turn** the dough out on a surface lightly dusted with rice flour, roll out thinly and use a 4 cm (1½ inch) cutter to cut out 20 cookies, rerolling the trimmings as necessary. Transfer to the prepared baking sheets and sprinkle with the flaked almonds.

**Place** in a preheated oven, 180°C (350°F), Gas Mark 4, for about 8 minutes until golden. Remove from the oven, leave for a few minutes to harden on the baking sheets, then transfer to a wire rack to cool.

**For coconut cookies**, make the dough as above, adding 50 g (2 oz) toasted desiccated coconut. Omit the orange rind and add a little extra egg yolk if the mixture is too dry. Roll into a long sausage shape, wrap in clingfilm and chill for 30 minutes. Cut thin slices of the dough, place on the prepared baking sheets and bake in the oven as above.

# orange animal biscuits

Preparation time **10 minutes**
Cooking time **10 minutes**
Makes **20**

200 g (7 oz) **brown rice flour**,
  plus extra for dusting
½ teaspoon **xanthan gum**
1 teaspoon **gluten-free
  baking powder**
50 g (2 oz) **butter**, cubed
50 g (2 oz) **soft light
  brown sugar**
grated rind of 1 **orange**
1 **egg**, beaten
2 tablespoons **golden syrup**

**To decorate**
150 g (5 oz) **icing sugar**
1 tablespoon **boiling water**
**food colouring** (optional)
**gluten-free sweets**

**Line** 2 baking sheets with nonstick baking paper.

**Place** the flour, xanthan gum, baking powder and butter in a food processor and whizz until the mixture resembles fine breadcrumbs. Alternatively, mix together the flour, xanthan gum and baking powder in a large bowl. Add the butter and rub in with the fingertips until the mixture resembles fine breadcrumbs. Stir in the sugar and orange rind.

**Add** the egg and golden syrup and combine to form a firm dough. Turn the dough out on a surface lightly dusted with rice flour, roll out to a thickness of 5 mm (¼ inch) and use animal cutters to cut out 20 biscuits, rerolling the trimmings as necessary. Transfer the biscuits to the prepared baking sheets.

**Place** in a preheated oven, 160°C (325°F), Gas Mark 3, for about 10 minutes until golden. Remove from the oven, leave for a few minutes on the baking sheets to harden, then transfer to a wire rack to cool.

**Mix** the icing sugar with the boiling water and add the colouring, if using, then smooth over the biscuits or pipe icing details. Decorate with sweets and leave to set.

**For jewelled Christmas cookies**, make the dough as above, then cut out shapes using Christmas cutters. Place the biscuits on the prepared baking sheets and make an indentation (or more than one, if liked) in the dough, making sure you don't push all the way through. Roughly crush different coloured gluten-free boiled sweets and put a few pieces into each indentation. Cook as above and gently dust with icing sugar once cooled.

# lemon, pistachio & fruit squares

Preparation time **10 minutes**, plus chilling
Cooking time **20 minutes**
Makes **15–20**

**butter**, for greasing
grated rind of 1 **lemon**
75 g (3 oz) **ready-to-eat dried dates**, chopped
75 g (3 oz) unsalted **pistachio nuts**, chopped
75 g (3 oz) **flaked almonds**, chopped
125 g (4 oz) **soft light brown sugar**
150 g (5 oz) **millet flakes**
40 g (1½ oz) **gluten-free cornflakes**, lightly crushed
400 g (13 oz) **can condensed milk**
25 g (1 oz) mixed **pumpkin** and **sunflower seeds**

**Grease** a 28 x 18 cm (11 x 7 inch) baking tin.

**Mix** together all the ingredients in a large bowl until well combined and spoon the mixture into the prepared tin.

**Place** in a preheated oven, 180°C (350°F), Gas Mark 4, for 20 minutes.

**Remove** from the oven and leave to cool in the tin. Mark into 15–20 squares and chill until firm. Store in an airtight container and eat wthin 3–5 days.

**For chocolate fruit & nut squares**, place 75 g (3 oz) gluten-free white chocolate and 75 g (3 oz) gluten-free plain dark chocolate in separate heatproof bowls over saucepans of simmering water and leave until melted. Drizzle over the cooked and cooled squares and leave to set.

# bite-sized mince pies

Preparation time **10 minutes**, plus chilling
Cooking time **15–20 minutes**
Makes **24**

150 g (5 oz) **rice flour**
2 tablespoons **polenta**
¼ teaspoon **ground cinnamon**
75 g (3 oz) **butter**, cubed
2 tablespoons **caster sugar**
grated rind of 1 **orange**
1 **egg yolk**
**icing sugar**, for dusting

**Filling**
400 g (13 oz) **gluten-free mincemeat**
1 tablespoon **brandy**
25 g (1 oz) **flaked almonds**, roughly chopped, plus extra to decorate
25 g (1 oz) **marzipan**, frozen and then grated

**Place** the flour, polenta, cinnamon and butter in a food processor and whizz until the mixture resembles fine breadcrumbs. Alternatively, mix together the flour, polenta and cinnamon in a large bowl. Add the butter and rub in with the finegrtips until the mixture resembles fine breadcrumbs. Stir in the sugar and orange rind.

**Add** the egg yolk and enough cold water to mix to a dough. Wrap in clingfilm and chill for 30 minutes.

**Roll** the pastry out gently between 2 pieces of cling-film to a thickness of 5 mm (¼ inch) and use a 6 cm (2½ inch) cutter to cut out 24 rounds, rerolling the trimmings as necessary. Use to line 2 x 12-hole mini-muffin trays, and patch any gaps with pastry trimmings.

**Mix** together the filling ingredients in a bowl, spoon into the pastry cases and crumble over any leftover pastry. Place in a preheated oven, 180°C (350°F), Gas Mark 4, for 15–20 minutes until golden.

**Remove** from the oven and leave to cool for a few minutes in the tins. Sprinkle with flaked almonds, then serve warm with a dusting of icing sugar and some brandy cream, if liked.

**For creamy mince pies**, beat together 2 tablespoons cream cheese and 1 tablespoon brandy, then spoon a little of this mixture into the pastry cases before topping with the mincemeat filling and pastry crumbs. Bake in the oven as above.

# index

# acknowledgements

**Executive Editor:** Eleanor Maxfield
**Editor:** Joanne Wilson
**Executive Art Editor:** Juliette Norsworthy
**Designer:** Penny Stock
**Photographer:** William Shaw
**Home economist:** Sara Lewis
**Proofreader:** Jo Richardson
**Props stylist:** Liz Hippisley
**Production Controller:** Caroline Alberti

**Special photography:** © Octopus Publishing Group Limited/William Shaw
**Other photography:** Fotolia/JJAVA 15; Octopus Publishing Group/Emma Neish 2, 4, 151, 153, 155, 157, 159, 163, 169, 185, 187, 193, 197, 199, 201, 203, 205, 207, 211, 213, 215, 217, 219, 221, 223, 225, 227, 229, 231, 233; /Lis Parsons 16, 92, 143; /Craig Robertson 23, 33, 51, 53, 63, 119, 123, 129, 139, 141, 161, 165; /William Shaw 14, 38, 166, 190, 208; /Ian Wallace 144.